SOUTH WEST ENGLAND'S COAST

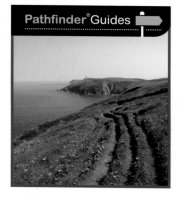

Pathfinder® Guides

Outstanding
Circular Walks

*Walks selected by
Sue Viccars*

Contents

South West Coast Path

Origins of coastal paths

Britain's south-west peninsula – from west Somerset and Dorset through Devon and into Cornwall – justifiably attracts thousands of visitors each year. For many the draw lies in the mix of sweeping moorland, wooded valleys, patchwork farmland, sparkling rivers, picturesque villages and pubs – not forgetting the equable climate, two National Parks and several Areas of Outstanding Natural Beauty. But for walkers specifically what gives the South West its edge is its beautiful and unique coastline, studded with atmospheric fishing villages and superb beaches, rugged cliffs and broad estuaries.

The 'jewel in the crown' is the South West Coast Path, Britain's longest National Trail, which stretches for 630 miles (1,015km) from Minehead on the edge of Exmoor National Park in Somerset to the shores of Poole Harbour in Dorset. It is likely that coastal paths have existed for many hundreds of years: Roman signal stations have been found on North Devon's cliffs, and Iron Age cliff castles dot the coastal footpath. But this remarkable and continuous coastal route has its real origins in the 18th century, when heavy duties on imported goods encouraged a lively tradition of smuggling via the sheltered coves and remote inlets. Customs and exise officers roamed the clifftops on the lookout, and in 1822 the Coastguard Service was set up in an attempt to control this illegal activity. The coastal paths were also used by 'huers', who alerted fishermen at sea as to the whereabouts of shoals of fish (hence 'hue and cry').

The Coast Path today

Today the Coast Path plays a rather different role as a fantastic route for walkers – and the good news is that you do not have to do it all at once! The path is easily accessible along its length, and the character of the coast amazingly varied (note that many newcomers to the Coast Path are taken aback at how strenuous sections can be). The 28 circular routes in this book – listed in an anti-clockwise direction – have been selected to give a broad range to suit all levels of ability and interest, from a stroll along the Fowey Estuary in south Cornwall to a tough 10½ miles (16.6km) on the spectacular coast of North Devon's Hartland Peninsula.

The Coast Path at
Widmouth Head, looking
towards Rillage Point,
North Devon

Exmoor & North Devon

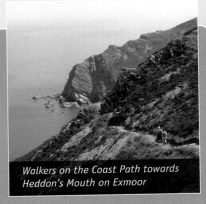

Walkers on the Coast Path towards Heddon's Mouth on Exmoor

There is no 'right way' to tackle the South West Coast Path, but the majority of people attempting to walk the full 630 miles (1,015km) tend to start in Minehead and walk in an anti-clockwise direction: and so the routes suggested in this book follow that lead. Exmoor National Park holds the first 34 miles (53km) of the Coast Path, which then runs through the North Devon AONB all the way from Combe Martin to the Cornish border. And whereas two thirds of the National Park lie within Somerset, the walker crosses into Devon at County Gate, giving the latter county two thirds of the Coast Path. This part of the Coast Path undeniably contains some of the finest cliff scenery in the country. Exmoor's famous hog's-back cliffs and high coastal hills (some of the highest in England are found on Holdstone Down, east of Combe Martin) give way to the most dramatic stretch of the Coast Path around Hartland Point. Razor-back reefs, sheer crags, hanging valleys and waterfalls, and an endless succession of steep-sided combes provide stiff challenges for any walker (and over the centuries have proved the downfall of many ships – the coast is peppered with the remains of wrecks). This section is also the least walked and remotest part of the Coast Path.

But there are less strenuous areas too. The broad estuary of the great Taw and Torridge rivers which flow into Barnstaple Bay supports one of the most significant sand dune systems in Europe at Braunton Burrows, through which runs the Coast Path: the UNESCO North Devon Biosphere Reserve, designated on account of its unique flora and fauna. And in the National Park can be found the extraordinary shingle ridge at Porlock, dating back 8,000 years and breached by the sea in 1996, necessitating a permanent Coast Path diversion a short distance inland.

This variety of coastal landscape provides the opportunity for some stunning routes, from a stroll around tranquil Fremington Quay, at one time the busiest port between Bristol and Land's End, or a wander along the cliffs above Croyde Bay to Baggy Point, to a hard walk above craggy Heddon's Mouth, one of the few inlets on this inhospitable coast, with wonderful views inland up the wooded Heddon Valley.

Hurlstone

Much of this walk is on land that was part of the Holnicote estate, formerly owned by the Acland family and given to the National Trust by Sir Richard Acland in 1944. The walk passes through three picturesque villages, and the countryside between them is some of the finest in Exmoor, combining a steep combe, open moorland and glorious woodland, with excellent views over the coast, the Vale of Porlock and inland to high Exmoor – the latter views dominated by Dunkery Beacon. The only climbing comes soon after the start: a lengthy, steady, and eventually very steep ascent along the side of Bossington Hill and up through Hurlstone Combe on to Selworthy Beacon – the finest of many fine viewpoints on a splendid and outstandingly attractive walk.

Bossington is an idyllic place: a collection of thatched cottages sheltering at the foot of the steep, wooded slopes of Bossington Hill on the northern edge of the Vale of Porlock, ½ mile (800m) from a beach and with a clear, sparkling stream running through it on its way to the sea. It is also an excellent walking centre.

Take the path that leads directly from the car park, at the footpath sign to Hurlstone and Selworthy, and cross a footbridge to a T-junction of paths. Turn left at a footpath sign to Hurlstone, by the stream on the left, following a path which curves right along the edge of woodland. After passing through a gate, the path starts to gradually climb between gorse and bracken, up to a stone indicating that this is the

Start	Bossington
Distance	6¼ miles (10km)
Height gain	1,150 feet (350m)
Approximate time	3½ hours
Route terrain	Coastal and woodland tracks; very steep ascent up Hurlstone Combe
Parking	NT car park at Bossington (honesty box); Bossington is signed off A39 at Selworthy, between Minehead and Porlock
Dog friendly	On leads on Coast Path (sheep)
OS maps	Landranger 181 (Minehead & Brendon Hills), Explorer OL9 (Exmoor)
GPS waypoints	SS 898 480
	Ⓐ SS 899 489
	Ⓑ SS 923 478
	Ⓒ SS 919 468
	Ⓓ SS 905 469
	Ⓔ SS 903 470

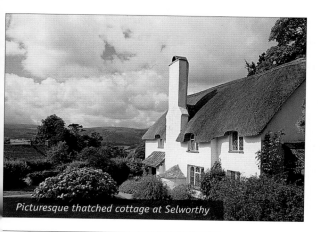

Picturesque thatched cottage at Selworthy

National Trust property of Hurlstone **A**.
From here there is a lovely view to the left across Porlock Bay to Porlock and Porlock Weir; ahead is the commanding headland of Hurlstone Point.

Turn right, following coastal path signs to Minehead, now climbing much more steeply through Hurlstone Combe, a cleft between Hurlstone Point on the left and Bossington Hill on the right. The long, steep haul to the head of the combe rewards you with magnificent views to the right across the Vale of Porlock to the thickly wooded valleys and moors beyond. Keep following Coast Path signs, ignoring all tracks to right and left. Where the Coast Path eventually bears left keep straight ahead along a track to climb Selworthy Beacon (1,012 feet/308m), from which point the views – especially those looking across the sea to the coast of South Wales and inland to Dunkery Beacon – are even more magnificent. Continue past the cairn, and keep right at a fork to descend to a road **B**. Keep ahead along the road, round a right-hand bend and then bear right, at a bridleway sign to Selworthy and Dunster, along a track, bearing right when you meet another track and heading gradually downhill. At the next footpath sign to Selworthy turn sharply to the right to continue more steeply downhill, curving through the beautiful woodland of Selworthy Combe, by a brook on the right, finally passing through a gate and on to a lane **C**.

To the left is Selworthy church, an imposing 14th- to 15th-century building, easily seen for miles around because of its distinctive white colour. It is periodically coated with a lime mixture to protect the stone from the weather – a practice that used to be more common in the past. The inside is particularly impressive for a small village church, with a fine, aisled nave and 18th-century gallery at its west end. From the south porch the view over the village to Dunkery is one of the finest in the area. Selworthy, which mainly comprises a number of thatched cottages grouped around a green, is remarkably picturesque and uniform – almost unreal in its perfection. It was purpose-built by the Aclands of nearby Holnicote in the early 19th century for their retired tenants and estate workers to live in.

Turn right by the cross in front of the church and walk across the charming and delightful Selworthy Green between the thatched cottages and **Periwinkle Cottage Tearooms**, rejoining the lane lower down to continue through the village. At the bottom end turn right along another lane, at a footpath sign to Allerford, passing a farm and continuing along a hedge-lined path to a fork. Here take the left-hand path, skirting woods on the right; down to a lane; continue straight on along the narrow lane which curves left to drop down to the ford, cottage and old pack-horse bridge at Allerford **D**. This must be one of the most photographed scenes in the country, adorning literally thousands of calendars, birthday cards and chocolate boxes – undeniably idyllic and nostalgic, the town-dweller's idealised view of rural life.

Cross the pack-horse bridge and turn right along the road through the village, turning right **E** again at the far end along the drive to Stoates Farm. Continue over

a footbridge and turn left along a shady path, at first keeping by the stream on the left. The path later bears right, uphill, along the edge of the delightful woodland of Allerford Plantation, bearing left on meeting another path at a footpath sign to Bossington. Immediately ahead is a fork: keep along the lower path and continue to reach a gate at a path junction. *Over to the left is Lynch Chapel – you can make a slight detour to visit it by turning left just before the gate, and continuing down to the road opposite the chapel.* This fine, unaltered 16th-century building belonged to Athelney Abbey up to the closure of the monasteries in the 1530s and is believed to have been the chapel of the manor of Bossington.

After passing through the gate continue across a field, go through a gap in the wire fence and turn left along the edge of the next field down to a gate. Go through, continue down the steps ahead and turn right along a path through woodland which descends to another gate. Go through that and bear left to cross the footbridge back into Bossington. ●

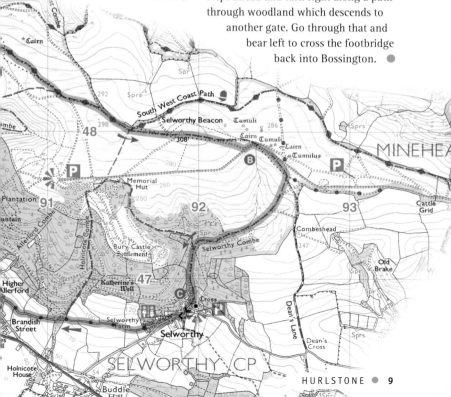

walk 2

Start
Woody Bay

Distance
5¾ miles (9km)

Height gain
1,410 feet (430m)

Approximate time
3½ hours

Route terrain
Non-rocky Coast Path, long steady ascents and descents, some damp areas in coastal woodland

P Parking
NT car park; follow signs for Woody Bay from A39 at Martinhoe Cross just east of Woody Bay Station, between Parracombe and Barbrook

Dog friendly
No problems; Coast Path exposed in places

OS maps
Landranger 180 (Barnstaple & Ifracombe), Explorer OL9 Exmoor)

GPS waypoints
SS 675 486
Ⓐ SS 673 486
Ⓑ SS 655 481
Ⓒ SS 654 487
Ⓓ SS 671 490

Woody Bay & The Beacon

Both outward and return routes of this circular walk stick to the coast, using both Coast Path and a Victorian carriage drive with magnificent views along Exmoor's cliffs and plentiful opportunities for spotting a good variety of seabirds.

From the parking area walk uphill; where the lane soon bears sharp left keep straight ahead Ⓐ onto a broad track, a former late Victorian carriageway (see later), signed to **Hunters Inn**. The track runs along the top of West Woodybay Wood, a designated SAC (Special Area of Conservation) for its sessile (hanging) oakwoods; the National Trust is doing extensive work in the Woody Bay area to control the spread of rhododendron, which can be seen dotting the cliffs later in this walk. The drive passes through a small gate and soon enters open country, dropping into the combe of the Hollow Brook and soon returning to the cliffs. Look out for a small path rising left to the site of The Beacon, a small round fort occupied from c AD50–74 by a garrison of 80 Roman soldiers on the lookout for attack from the Silures of South Wales.

Follow the track on eventually to meet the edge of Heddon's Mouth Cleave, and turn inland, with stunning views over the steep-sided wooded valley ahead; the Coast Path to Combe Martin runs 500 feet (150m) above the other side of the Cleave. The track descends gently, crossing Hill Brook, and continues to descend to meet a junction of paths Ⓑ. *For an ice cream from the NT shop or refreshments at The Hunters Inn keep straight ahead.*

To continue turn sharp right, following the bridleway, which descends towards the Heddon River. Undulate along the right bank, keeping left at a fork along a pretty riverside path, to meet a bridge and the Coast Path Ⓒ. Do not cross the river, but follow the track straight ahead. The track ascends slightly as the landscape starts to open up; reach a junction and bear right on the Coast Path, signed Woody Bay, on a narrow path that ascends steadily up the east side of the valley. Pass through an area of bracken and cross Hill Brook. Soon the beach at rocky Heddon's Mouth – a rare inlet on this inhospitable coast – and the restored 19th-century double limekiln, last used in 1870, comes into view below. Charcoal and gorse were burned in the lower chamber, with limestone and culm (from South Wales) layered above, to produce quicklime, used to fertilise Exmoor's acid soils. The beach was last used commercially in the Second World War for the export of timber which was used in the mines of South Wales.

Reach Highveer Point and enjoy wonderful views west towards the coast towards Widmouth Head near Ilfracombe and east to The Foreland beyond Lynmouth. The Coast Path – this section remarkably even underfoot – runs east towards Little and then Great Burland Rocks, then drops past the 656-foot/200-m waterfall in Hollow Brook Combe (wet underfoot) to gain spectacular views over the rocky coastal formations at Wringapeak (look for razorbills and guillemots in summer),

with Woody Bay and Gothic Lee Abbey beyond. Woody Bay has an interesting history: Martinhoe Manor estate was bought by 'Colonel' Benjamin Greene Lake in 1885, who planned to turn it into an upmarket resort but he went bankrupt and was imprisoned for fraud, and the estate was purchased by the National Trust in 1965.

The Coast Path enters West Woodybay Wood, soon passing through a gate, and eventually meets a lane on a hairpin bend just above Martinhoe Manor (originally Wooda Bay House, built in 1859). The Coast Path bears left downhill; take the right fork **D** and follow the lane uphill, climbing steadily to reach a T-junction. Turn right to the parking area. ●

walk 3

Start

Heddon's Gate

Distance

6¾ miles (10.8km)

Height gain

1,490 feet (455m)

Approximate time

4 hours

Route terrain

Woodland tracks, moorland, uneven Coast Path, long and steep descent to finish

Parking

NT car park (honesty box)/laneside parking at Heddon's Gate, signed off A399 between Blackmoor Gate and Combe Martin

Dog friendly

To be kept on leads on Coast Path (sheep)

OS maps

Landranger 180 (Barnstaple & Ilfracombe), Explorer OL9 (Exmoor)

GPS waypoints

SS 655 481
Ⓐ SS 638 475
Ⓑ SS 635 469
Ⓒ SS 625 476
Ⓓ SS 627 478
Ⓔ SS 649 491
Ⓕ SS 652 482

Trentishoe Down & Heddon's Mouth Cleave

Heddon's Mouth is one of Exmoor's few accessible coves, the haunt of smugglers in the 18th and 19th centuries. Although just a short stroll along the valley from Heddon's Gate, it's best appreciated from the Coast Path, which runs high above. This walk crosses lofty Trentishoe Down and follows the spectacular coast before encountering the sessile oak woodlands of the Heddon Valley.

Walk towards the **Hunters Inn** – the original thatched inn, popular in Victorian times with students from Oxford and Cambridge universities on walking tours, burned down in 1895 (see later) – passing to its left on Josey's Lane, soon crossing the Heddon River. Just before the next bridge over the Blackmoor Water turn left through a gate on a bridlepath/permitted path. Reach a junction of footpaths and turn right to pass to the left of a pretty cottage and cross a stream to meet another path. Turn left along the level track through woodland; at a fork follow the lower (left) path, which descends alongside an old wall to meet a lane; turn left.

After a few yards turn right as signed on a rocky footpath (signed Ladies Mile). Climb very steeply through woodland to a footpath junction on the edge of Trentishoe Down. Turn left Ⓐ on Ladies Mile, a lovely narrow path along the top edge of woodland. The path eventually leads to Trentishoe Manor, at one time the rectory; it is said that the Ladies Mile was constructed so that the ladies of the manor could walk to church at Trentishoe (see later). Where you spot a lane below left, look for a narrow path bearing off right uphill and turn right **B**, leaving Ladies Mile. It's a pretty steady uphill climb, with the occasional short level stretch. Eventually rise above the woodland into bracken and gorse on a broad grassy path, parallel to a drystone wall left; where the wall bears away 90 degrees left, keep straight ahead uphill, passing to the right of a big stand of gorse. Meet a rough track by a small post and keep ahead uphill. Follow the track over the edge of Trentishoe Down, home to a group of Bronze Age barrows; it levels off to meet a road, to the left of The Glass House, an unusual contemporary building with huge windows. Just to the west can be seen the swell of Holdstone Down, the highest coastal hill in the south-west, rising to

1,145 feet (349m) above Exmoor's famous rugged hog's-back cliffs.

Turn right **C** and walk along the lane, descending gently, with fabulous views towards the cliffs on the east side of Heddon's Mouth and The Beacon. At the first parking area on the left (the lane ahead descends and bears right), bear left **D** through it to find a broad grassy path which passes two benches and continues down-hill to meet the Coast Path.

Turn right and follow the Coast Path

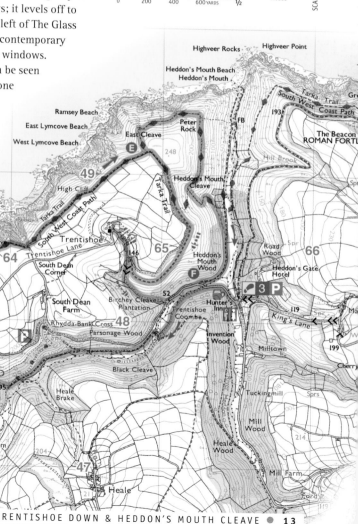

SCALE 1:25000 or 2½ INCHES to 1 MILE 4CM to 1KM

downhill (rocky underfoot), with stunning views ahead. At the next fork keep straight on (right). Pass through a gate and continue across an area of grassland, to pass through another gate above Neck Wood. Continue alongside a bank, soon passing through a gate to clip the edge of a field; then through another.

Keep ahead, eventually to meet a footpath post and follow the Coast Path left . *For an alternative finish – and if you want to visit St Peter's Church at Trentishoe – turn right here along a glorious path which runs high above the Heddon Valley to meet the lane*

Lamb on the Coast Path

just below the church; turn right uphill. There are records of a church here as long ago as 1260, and it's well worth a visit for its squat, castellated tower and 18th-century minstrel's gallery; there are rumours that smugglers' contraband was at one time hidden in the tower. To finish follow the lane downhill into Trentishoe Combe, turning left on meeting the lane to rejoin the route at ❻. The Coast Path narrows and becomes quite exposed, and rocky in places, before turning sharp right at Peter Rock above Heddon's Mouth. Down on the rocky beach below is an unusual restored 19th-century double limekiln. The path runs inland up the Heddon Valley, later dropping across an area of scree (the result of intense

freeze–thaw activity on the underlying sandstone during the Ice Age), then zigzags steeply downhill to enter woodland. Pass through a small gate, and continue downhill to meet a broad track. Turn right and keep ahead along the valley bottom to meet a lane through a kissing-gate.

Turn left ❻; turn left to pass Harry's Orchard (stocked with traditional English varieties, and open to the public) and the Heddon River to return to your car. Hunters Inn was bought by Benjamin Green Lake in 1885; by summer 1895 Lake had constructed the carriage drive from here to Woody Bay. After the disastrous fire the hotel was rebuilt in Swiss chalet style in 1897, and continues to flourish to this day. ●

Berrynarbor & Widmouth Head

Delightful Berrynarbor – a frequent best-kept village winner – sits in hilly country a mile (1.5km) from the coast near Ilfracombe. A climb out of the pretty Sterridge Valley and a gentle descent into Hele is followed by one of the least strenuous – but lovely – stretches of North Devon's coastal footpath: just one lengthy stepped up and down to encounter.

walk 4

Start
Berrynarbor

Distance
7 miles (11.1km)

Height gain
1,265 feet (385m)

Approximate time
3½ hours

Route terrain
Hilly fields and tracks, undulating coast path, quiet lanes

Parking
Parking at Berrynarbor community shop; ¾ mile (1.2km) off A399 between Ilfracombe and Combe Martin

Dog friendly
To be kept on leads through fields; non-dog-friendly stiles

OS maps
Landranger 180 (Barnstaple & Ilfracombe), Explorers 139 (Bideford, Ilfracombe & Barnstaple) or OL9 (Exmoor)

GPS waypoints
SS 561 466
Ⓐ SS 553 458
Ⓑ SS 545 461
Ⓒ SS 534 466
Ⓓ SS 535 476
Ⓔ SS 557 480
Ⓕ SS 561 478

From the car park turn left, then left at the junction opposite St Peter's Church; take the first lane left, soon passing the school. Pass the junction at 'Turn Round' and continue downhill; where a footpath goes right, take a raised path on the left through a gate, then a meadow, and another gate to rejoin the lane. Keep ahead over Rock Hill into the Sterridge Valley. The maker of Berrynarbor's famous flowerpot men (seen all over the village) lives at Hillside Cottage, soon passed.

Where the lane bears sharp left (Lower Farm Rows left) bear right through a kissing-gate on a footpath Ⓐ. Climb steadily, then follow the top left edge of a big field. At the end pass a willow clump; do not follow the obvious path, but bear slightly right along the left edge of the next field. At the end cross a stile into a wood. Cross two small streams, then a footbridge/stile into a field; turn left along the bottom edge. Where the fence bears away keep straight ahead uphill, cutting off the corner. At the top cross a stile, and bear diagonally right across the field: as you crest the top aim for a footpath post in the far hedge. Cross two stiles onto a lane opposite the entrance to Lower Trayne Farm Ⓑ.

Follow the drive downhill. The path is well signed through farm buildings: cross the yard and through a gate to the right of stables. Keep ahead through another gate; turn left through another and follow the track, bearing right downhill into the valley. Pass through a gate and keep ahead, dropping gently to the bottom left corner by Comyn Wood. A gate leads to a woodland path (muddy). Reach Comyn Farm and cross the stream (no footbridge): bear left through a gate between houses, then bear right to a junction.

Turn right Ⓒ, almost immediately turning left through a gate on a narrow hedged path, (Cat Lane), eventually meeting a track via a gate on a bend. Keep ahead, gently downhill, to a T-junction with houses opposite. Turn right to meet a narrow lane on a bend; turn right. Just round the bend turn left (signs for the Old Cornmill). Go through the gates and pass between the mill and tearoom. The path eventually meets the road at Hele **D**.

Cross the road with care; turn right. After about ¼ mile (400m) bear left on the Coast Path onto Hagginton Point: cross the parking area and continue for 150 yards up the roadside verge; the path then runs parallel to the road, behind a hedge. Bear left at the next Coast Path post, eventually reaching coastguard cottages; turn left to walk around Rillage Point. Cross a stile in woodland at the back of Samson's Bay; emerge from the trees and continue to cross a stile; turn left and walk uphill on a narrow path towards the sea. Descend then climb a long flight of steps onto Widmouth Head. Descend another long flight, and enjoy views along the Exmoor coast. Pass the entrance to Widmouth Farm and cross a stile; continue up a fenced path. Turn left at the top on a wooded path that descends gently. *For about an hour either side of very high tide the*

foreshore at Water Mouth is impassable: if so turn right onto the road where indicated, and follow it downhill. The Coast Path descends to the foreshore. Turn right, soon bearing left beneath the harbour wall; turn right to leave the beach and go through a gate *(high water route rejoins)*. Follow the

Water Mouth viewed from the Coast Path

Coast Path left along the verge.

About 50 yards later turn left on a path that parallels the road. Re-emerge on the road at the harbour entrance; 50 yards later turn left **E** to leave the road again and pass through a gate into Watermouth Valley Camping Park. Keep ahead, meeting a driveway on a bend; bear left uphill. Where the drive ends keep straight on to exit the camping area by a Coast Path post. The path climbs steeply above Broad Strand to meet a track through a gate; turn right,

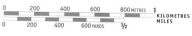

leaving the Coast Path **F** *(for a visit to the beach turn left and descend 227 steps!)*. Walk down the lane to the A399. Turn right briefly; cross over and take the lane to Berrynarbor, eventually climbing steeply to pass the **Old Globe** and church; go right for the car park. ●

walk 5

Morte Point

Start
Mortehoe

Distance
7½ miles (12km)

Height gain
1,885 feet (575m)

Approximate time
4 hours

Route terrain
Farmland, wooded valley, Coast Path (steep ascents/descents)

Parking
Car park at Mortehoe (pay & display): Mortehoe is signed off B3343 (off A361 at Mullacott Cross between Braunton and Ilfracombe)

Dog friendly
To be kept on leads through fields; some non-dog-friendly stiles

OS maps
Landranger 180 (Barnstaple & Ilfracombe), Explorer 139 (Bideford, Ilfracombe & Barnstaple)

GPS waypoints

SS 457 452
Ⓐ SS 465 455
Ⓑ SS 472 456
Ⓒ SS 482 452
Ⓓ SS 483 463
Ⓔ SS 479 464
Ⓕ SS 475 467
Ⓖ SS 462 467
Ⓗ SS 453 449

A medieval farmstead, rolling unimproved grassland, an ancient wooded valley, a secluded cove, a lighthouse, some of North Devon's oldest and most dangerous rocks off Morte Point, the death of many a ship ... this classic walk has it all. This deservedly popular section of Coast Path enjoys a succession of ascents and descents – and glorious wildflowers in spring.

Take the lane opposite the car park, signed to Lee, to pass North Morte Farm campsite. Where the way ahead is barred by a gate marked 'Bull Point Lighthouse', take the footpath to the right of a gate to the right. Pass through the campsite at Easewell on a tarmac way. Cross a parking area, and follow footpath signs ahead between buildings. Look carefully for a narrow concrete path that drops between the buildings left. Follow this to pass a pond and cross a stile into a field. Bear slightly left then right uphill to pass through a gate at Yarde Farm.

Turn left Ⓐ, almost immediately crossing a stile. The track bears right, reduces to a hedged path and ascends shallow steps. Cross a stile into a field, and follow the left edge. Pass through a small gate towards the end, drop to cross a stile, and keep along the left edge of the next. Cross a stile/gate at the end to meet a farm drive on a bend. Bear left; follow the drive towards buildings at atmospheric Damage Barton, dating from the mid-17th century (but there is evidence of a dwelling here in medieval times). Keep a look out for

footpath arrows and follow the track past the farmhouse. On reaching a junction of paths turn right **B**, and follow the track slightly uphill, with a wall right. At the T-junction turn left; just before meeting a big gate turn sharp right (unsigned) along a grassy path, bearing left through a gate after about 100 yards. Bear right; walk gently uphill, aiming for a footpath post. Turn right up a broad open track to another post. Keep ahead along the track to pass through a gate and cross a field. Aim for a footpath post on a small hillock ahead; pass to the left of it (with hedgebank left) to meet a small gate. Go through the gate, then bear half-right across the next field, aiming for a footpath post/stile onto a lane.

Cross the lane and stile into a field, then bear slightly right, soon crossing a stile into Borough Wood. Descend steeply under beech trees to a

T-junction; turn left **C**, almost immediately crossing a stile, and follow the path gently downhill for ¾ mile (1.2km) (muddy in parts). At the bottom of the wood meet a path junction and turn right over a footbridge/stile; cross the field and stile onto a narrow path (**The Grampus Inn** is a short detour right).

Turn left **D**; follow the path to join a narrow tarmac lane, which meets the lane and sea wall at Lee Bay. Known locally as 'Fuchsia Valley' for its wealth of wildflowers, Lee has some lovely 16th/17th cottages, but was notorious for smuggling in the 18th and 19th centuries. Turn left **E** to pass Smugglers Cottage. *Note that there is an alternative low-tide route: follow a concrete walkway across the beach, aiming for a cleft in the rocks on the*

SCALE 1:25000 or 2½ INCHES to 1 MILE 4CM to 1KM

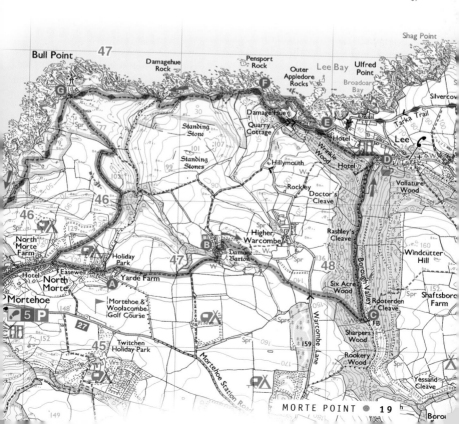

MORTE POINT ● **19**

Sandy Cove, with Lee Bay beyond

left-hand side: *follow the path carefully through the rocks (steps cut in places) to reach Sandy Cove. Walk across and up steep steps to rejoin the route* **F**.
The lane climbs very steeply past splendid houses; turn right on the Coast Path through a gate. The path descends steps to meet the alternative from Sandy Cove **F**.

Now follows a delightful section of Coast Path, with a succession of ascents and descents, but none very long. Drop into a combe to cross a footbridge, then zigzag up the other side through gorse. A level section ends at a stile and a steep descent into the next combe, with wonderful views (note that parts of the path are quite badly eroded). Cross a stream on a footbridge, then a stile, and zigzag uphill again.

A lovely level stretch across downland follows; pass Bull Point, then descend to pass to the left of the lighthouse wall (built 1879, demanned in 1995) and reach the entrance **G**. *For a shortcut turn left here and follow the road for 1 mile (1.6km) back to*

Mortehoe. Keep ahead up steps and continue on the Coast Path, soon negotiating another combe and a long stepped ascent. Pass a post at Windy Lag then descend to Rockham Bay (access to beach). Cross a stile/gate behind the beach, then ascend steps. At the next stile Mortehoe is signed left; keep ahead. Pass another footpath to Mortehoe and cross a stile, and ascend a long flight of steps. Enjoy views to Lundy and the turbulent waters off Morte Point around the Morte Stone; keep an eye out for grey seals in summer, which return to Lundy in winter to breed. Eventually rocky Morte Point – a jagged confusion of saw-toothed Morte Slates – is reached, carpeted with pink thrift in early summer.

The Coast Path runs on more smoothly towards the edge of Woolacombe. Follow signs along the cliffs to reach a path junction above Grunta Beach and turn left, signed Mortehoe **H**. Climb steeply uphill to reach the road through a gate; turn left to walk through Mortehoe to the car park.

Braunton Marsh & Burrows

Start
Velator Quay, Braunton

Distance
6¼ miles (10km)

Height gain
Negligible

Approximate time
2½ hours

Route terrain
Level coastal path, field tracks, country lanes; note no shade on route

Parking
At Velator Quay; Velator/Braunton Burrows signed off A361 on the Barnstaple side of Braunton

Dog friendly
Non-dog friendly stiles on Coast Path along River Caen

OS maps
Landranger 180 (Barnstaple & Ilfracombe), Explorer 139 (Bideford, Ilfracombe & Barnstaple)

GPS waypoints
SS 484 354
Ⓐ SS 480 344
Ⓑ SS 469 330
Ⓒ SS 464 326
Ⓓ SS 464 355
Ⓔ SS 474 357
Ⓕ SS 476 355
Ⓖ SS 484 359

This lengthy yet level walk explores the heart of the North Devon Biosphere Reserve, designated in 2002 on account of the area's rare plants and continuous human use from ancient times. The Coast Path follows the River Caen to meet the Taw; the return passes Braunton Burrows, one of Europe's most important dune systems, and traverses Braunton's medieval Great Field.

Velator Quay – today the haunt of pleasure craft – dates from 1853, when deepening of the River Caen enabled ships of up to 130 tons to access it. It was a thriving port, and an important lime-burning centre, until the arrival of the railway in 1874.

Embankments constructed in the 19th century to protect Braunton Marshes from the influx of tidal waters today provide pleasant walking routes; pick up the Coast Path from the southern end of the parking area (by the information board) and follow it along the embankment above the River Caen, soon crossing a stone stile. Cross another by the tollhouse (the road to Broad Sands below right is private), and keep ahead, with tidal mudflats left and views over the marshes to the right – grazing cattle, yellow flags, small stone linhays (shelters for livestock) – and glimpses of the dunes of Braunton Burrows, in places rising to almost 100 feet (30m) high, beyond.

Reach a footpath junction Ⓐ at the north end of Horsey Island (an area of reclaimed marshland); the original route of the Coast Path, which runs along the edge of the water, is no longer passable, so instead pick up the path that runs above the lane along the top of The Great Bank, crossing three stone stiles, with great views across the Taw/Torridge confluence to Appledore.

Drop onto the lane just before reaching the White House (landing place for the old Appledore ferry) and keep ahead to re-meet the Coast Path Ⓑ. *It is possible at low tide to walk along the beach, eventually turning right through the parking area to rejoin the recommended route at the entrance to Braunton Burrows.* Turn right and walk through a broad parking area, passing an information board at the end to enter Braunton Burrows, internationally renowned on account of its rare and diverse flora and fauna: Braunton parish boasts more species of flowering plant than any other in England. Follow the track ahead through low-growing vegetation to meet a Coast Path post.

Turn right **C** and follow the track for about 1¼ miles (2km) between the dunes and marshes. Originally the old way to the ferry, this track – known as 'the American Road' – was widened and straightened in the Second World War when the area was used for military amphibious training exercises in preparation for D-Day. Today it is the least interesting part of this walk; look out for cyclists (this section is both Coast Path and Tarka Trail). Pass an area of open water (left), beyond which the Coast Path is signed left; keep straight ahead to pass a parking area, and onto Sandy Lane.

Take the first lane right **D**. You find yourself in a very un-Devon landscape: a lane running straight ahead across Braunton Marsh, more reminiscent of the Somerset Levels! Pass Willowfield Lake Cottages, soon after bearing left on the lane to cross Sir Arthur's Pill (drainage channel). At the next right bend keep ahead up a hedged track *(if impassable due to deep water, stay on the lane, which bears 90 degrees right; at the next right bend, keep ahead on a path to rejoin the main route at* **F***)*; 200 yards later turn right **E** on a public footpath and walk along the right edge of a field. At the next footpath junction turn left **F** and follow a track through the middle of Braunton Great Field – a remnant of the medieval open strip field system, with many field names dating from that time – to reach a T-junction of tracks. Turn right, immediately bearing left on

High water at Velator Quay

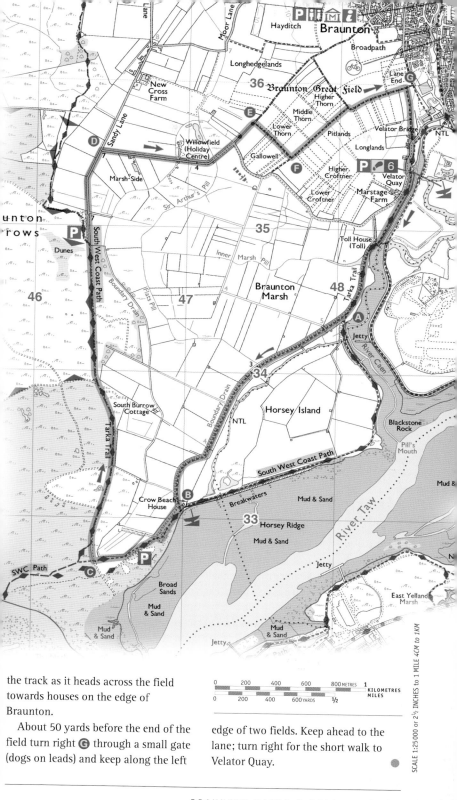

the track as it heads across the field towards houses on the edge of Braunton.

About 50 yards before the end of the field turn right **G** through a small gate (dogs on leads) and keep along the left edge of two fields. Keep ahead to the lane; turn right for the short walk to Velator Quay.

Fremington Quay

Start
Fremington Quay

Distance
3 miles (4.8km)

Height gain
Negligible

Approximate time
1½ hours

Route terrain
Level tracks and field paths

P Parking
Designated parking area at Fremington Quay, signed off B3233 at Fremington, 2½ miles (4km) west of Barnstaple

OS maps
Landranger 180 (Barnstaple & Ilfracombe), Explorer 139 (Bideford, Ilfracombe & Barnstaple)

GPS waypoints
✎ SS 517 334
Ⓐ SS 517 340
Ⓑ SS 520 335
Ⓒ SS 527 334
Ⓓ SS 522 329
Ⓔ SS 520 326

Fremington Quay, once the busiest port between Bristol and Land's End, dates from the 1840s when silting of the Taw Estuary prevented large vessels from reaching Barnstaple. Today the line of the old North Devon Railway carries cyclists and walkers through this delightful spot. This easy walk follows the Tarka Trail along the Taw before returning along tranquil Fremington Pill.

From the end of the parking area pick up a small path under trees (just left of the drive to Railway Cottage) onto the foreshore. Walk along the foreshore to reach an abandoned limekiln on the right. The Taw Vale Railway & Dock Company was formed in 1838 to build a deep-water quay at Fremington, and a horse-drawn line to Barnstaple was constructed. In 1854, when the main North Devon Railway line reached Barnstaple, and the line to Bideford via Fremington further developed the following year, the Quay's fortunes received another boost. Lime and coal were landed here from South Wales (and vast amounts of ball clay from Merton and Petersmarland in Mid Devon exported) and burned locally to produce fertiliser to aid local farmers. William Thorne, a local industrialist, was chairman of the company: his house, built in 1872, now houses the Barnstaple & North Devon Museum.

Just past the limekiln turn right Ⓐ on a hedged track, which soon bears right, and eventually reaches a bridge over the Tarka Trail. Do not cross the bridge, but bear right Ⓑ down steps onto the Trail. Turn left under the bridge (watch out for bikes) and continue along the old railway line through a long cutting – look out for blue field scabious and meadow brown butterflies in summer – eventually to emerge into open country with extensive saltmarsh and mudflats leading to the River Taw on the left (the Taw Estuary provides important habitats for a wide range of specialised plants and wildlife, and is a huge wintering ground for migrant birds). In summer look out for sea lavender and sea aster (one of the few plants that can cope with immersion in seawater, and which helps stabilise the marshes).

After just under ½ mile (800m) look for a footpath sign right, and turn right Ⓒ down steps to cross a stile and boardwalk. Walk up a gently ascending hedged grassy track to meet another at Clampitt; turn right. The track soon bears sharp left to meet a lane on a corner, opposite a thatched cottage. Turn right; about 75 yards later turn left Ⓓ on a public footpath on a grassy path (damp underfoot after rain) to emerge into a field. Follow the left edge to pass through a hedge gap and continue in the same direction: the waters of Fremington Pill – once navigable to its head at Muddlebridge (before the building of Fremington Quay a local port operated from the Pill) – come into view ahead. At the field end drop to cross a stile onto a lane.

Turn right **E** and follow the narrow lane back along the Pill towards the quay (it can be busy at peak times, but drivers are warned of walkers' presence and limited to 15mph). The lane bears sharp right; just before meeting houses (right) turn left at the edge of a small parking area on a concrete path that leads to the Tarka Trail, and turn right. About 25 yards later turn left to walk along the edge of the quay, eventually turning left at the end to the car park.

The Tarka Trail crosses Fremington Pill on the old railway bridge

The railway closed in the 1960s, and the last ship to visit Fremington was the Dutch merchant vessel *Dec* in 1969. Although all but the old station and signal box have been demolished (now housing a Heritage Centre and **café**) you can still see the outline of the platform, and the depth of the waters off the quay. From the 17th to 19th centuries Fremington was also known for the Fremington Pottery, based on the discovery locally of a seam of plastic fine-grained clay. Functional pots, and a few decorative pieces, were exported from Fremington to Wales, Ireland, France and the New World. ●

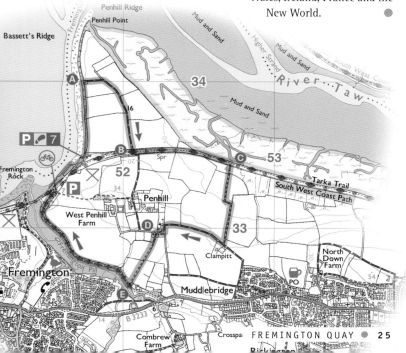

Start

Rocket House,
Hartland Quay

Distance

10½ miles (16.6km)

Height gain

2,230 feet (680m)

Approximate time

6 hours

Route terrain

Strenuous Coast Path
with many steep
ascents and descents:
inland route undulating
green lanes and tracks

Parking

Extensive parking area
(fee-paying in season)
above Hartland Quay,
2½ miles (4km) west
of Hartland village

Dog friendly

To be kept on leads
through fields

OS maps

Landranger 180
(Barnstaple &
Ilfracombe), Explorer
139 (Bideford,
Ilfracombe &
Barnstaple)

GPS waypoints

 SS 226 247
Ⓐ SS 230 266
Ⓑ SS 233 275
Ⓒ SS 235 273
Ⓓ SS 232 262
Ⓔ SS 235 246
Ⓕ SS 231 218
Ⓖ SS 223 218
Ⓗ SS 227 233
Ⓙ SS 223 246

Hartland Point & Speke's Mill Mouth

The remote Hartland peninsula – Ptolemy's Promontory of Hercules – is Devon's most north-westerly point, and holds the toughest section of the South West Coast Path. This route encounters a succession of steep-sided combes, rocky bays and magnificent coastal scenery – and a wonderful feeling of space. Inland green lanes provide pleasant walking past Hartland Abbey and Docton Mill, perfectly placed for tea.

From the car park entrance (toll booth) pass through a gate by the Rocket House. Follow the Coast Path along the cliffs *(take care)* above Hartland Quay, dating from 1586 – when inland communications were almost non-existent – and active until the late 19th century when the quay was destroyed by the sea. Descend into the valley, turning inland to a junction; turn left across the Abbey River. Pass behind Blackpool Mill Cottage (location for the TV drama *Sense & Sensibility*) to a track.

Turn left then climb very steeply right uphill (steps). At the top pass through a gate and turn right, bearing left at the next post along Blegberry Cliff: the contorted rocks along this coast are a geologist's dream. Descend across a stile and head downhill. The path drops rockily to cross a stream in a steep-sided flower-filled gorge above Blegberry beach. Ascend steeply; soon descend into Smoothlands via an eroded path. At

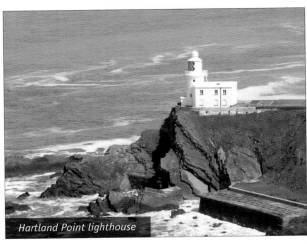

Hartland Point lighthouse

the end of the valley rise to a footpath junction and follow the left edge of a big field, eventually passing through a gate; follow the Coast Path left **A** at the next junction.

Descend uneven steps into the next combe; cross a stream before bearing back to the coast. At the next post bear right to climb steeply onto Upright Cliff, eventually with a wire fence right. The path levels on Blagdon Cliff. Where the wire fence ends bear left along the cliff edge, passing through gorse and along the left edge of the next field: a memorial (left) to the torpedoed *Glenart Castle* affords views over Hartland Point lighthouse (erected 1874) and, on a clear day, to Lundy. Continue up the field, and along the left edge of the

next. Follow the Coast Path right to meet a track by the lighthouse gates.

Turn right **B** through a parking area at Shipload Bay, passing the **Point@ Hartland** (seasonal café); bear right up the access road past Lundy's helicopter terminal. Where the road bears sharp left keep ahead **C** to descend through

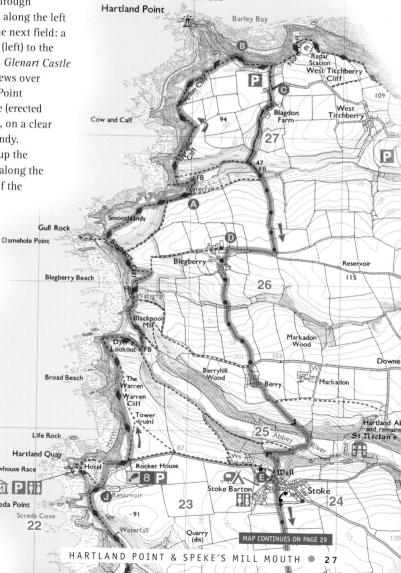

Green lane to Blegberry

the broad green lane ahead into and out of a valley to reach Wargery Farm; turn right on the farm drive to a lane junction at Kernstone Cross. Follow the lane ahead, dropping steeply to the crossroads at Lymebridge. Keep straight on (Docton Mill and Gardens right, **tearoom**) steeply uphill, levelling off and passing Milford Cross. Pass Lower Elmscott Farm; where the lane bears sharp left, with Post Box Cottage right, keep ahead on a signed

Blagdon Farm. The track passes through a gate and continues downhill along the right edge of a field, and through another gate. Meet a junction; turn left to cross a stream into woodland. Cross a footbridge and walk steadily up a green lane to reach a broad track, and bear left; eventually pass through a gate, bearing right to a lane. Turn right.

At the entrance to Blegberry Farm turn left **D** (unsigned) down a drive. Where that bears right keep ahead on a green lane that descends steeply then rises to pass through a big gate to meet a lane on a corner; keep straight ahead past buildings at Berry. Descend into the Abbey Valley, with views to Hartland Abbey (dating from 1157: the present house was rebuilt in 1779); climb steeply uphill into Stoke by St Nectan's Church with its landmark tower, at 128 feet (39m) the highest in Devon (toilets).

Turn left **E**; almost immediately turn right (by Church House) on a tarmac lane. Where it bears sharp left follow concrete way **F**.

The hedged track eventually passes along the left edge of fields and through a gateway into a field. Bear diagonally left, aiming for the far corner, and through a gate onto the Coast Path.

Turn right **G** along massive cliffs. Pass through a gate and along the seaward edge of a wire fence *(precipitous)*; cross a stile and go through a gate, soon passing a bench on the cliff edge. Cross a stile; soon meet a post, with the Coast Path signed right (valley route), and keep ahead on the cliff-top path over Swansford Hill, with a deep valley right. Towards the end of the hill wonderful views of steep-sided St Catherine's Tor and Hartland Quay appear ahead. The path starts to descend along a narrow ridge *(take care)*; look right a to spot a Coast Path post on the track in the valley. Drop right and aim for that post, picking up another en route where the alternative paths re-join; turn left across the stream on a

footbridge,
and ascend to
the track.

Turn left **H** and follow the
track towards Speke's Mill Mouth; note
the waterfall left. At the next Coast Path
post turn right to zigzag steeply out of
the combe to pass through a gate.
Descend, soon bearing inland to pass
through a gate. Walk towards the right
edge of St Catherine's Tor; cross a
stream on stepping stones and bear left
to pass through a hedgebank gap. Keep

ahead to find a rising track, which bears
left round the hill; pass through a gate,
then walk left towards Hartland Quay.
At the next Coast Path post **J** turn left
for the Quay and **hotel**; to complete the
walk keep ahead across the parking
area to meet a lane. Cross over; turn
right to find the Coast Path, which rises
steeply to the Rocket House. ●

Cornwall

9 Hawker Country
Rolling farmland and strenuous Coast Path
4¾ miles (7.6km)
3 hours

10 Dizzard Point
Very strenuous Coast Path, fields and woodland
8¼ miles (13.2km)
4½ hours

11 Tintagel & Boscastle
Coast Path, rolling farmland and wooded river valley
10 miles (16km)
5½ hours

12 Stepper Point from Trevone
Moderate Coast Path, fields and farm tracks
7¼ miles (11.5km)
3½ hours

13 Porthcurno & Porthgwarra
Undulating Coast Path, fields and farm tracks
5 miles (7.9km)
2½ hours

14 Lizard Point
Moderate Coast Path, tracks across Lizard Downs
7¾ miles (12.5km)
4 hours

15 Polruan
River valley woodland, lanes, moderate Coast Path
5 miles (8.2km)
2½ hours

16 Looe & Talland Bay
Wooded riverside path, fields, undemanding Coast Path
7½ miles (12km)
4 hours

Padstow Bay

Cornwall

West Looe

Cornwall may only measure 80 miles (129km) from the Tamar River (the Devon border) to Land's End, but the county has an astonishing 300 miles (483km) of coastline from north of Bude to the Rame Peninsula on the south coast. Cornwall experiences the mildest climate in the country, with around 1,500 hours of sunshine per year – but the weather is unpredictable, and conditions can be markedly different on north and south coasts, only 11 miles (17.7km) apart at the narrowest point in West Penwith. The landscape also differs remarkably: the walker can choose between the wild and rugged north, where old fishing villages can be found in occasional inlets and the prevailing westerly winds and seas hammer the cliffs, or the softer wooded river valleys and creeks of the south, beloved of the sailing fraternity, with historic seafaring centres such as Fowey and Looe. The county is known too for its fantastic beaches, from long expanses of sand backed by lofty dune systems to tiny rocky coves, where all manner of marine life can be found stranded in rockpools at low tide.

Man's influence on the coastal areas over the centuries can be found in the form of standing stones and megalithic quoits, and coastal fortifications – Iron Age cliff castles, 13th-century remains at Tintagel and south coast defences built during the reign of Henry VIII – and the remnants of the tin-mining industry, represented by a proliferation of engine houses and chimneys. Much of the coast – the far south-west in particular – is part of the Cornwall & West Devon World Heritage Mining site, designated in 2007. The heavily fragmented Cornwall AONB also covers a good percentage of the coast, including Land's End and the Lizard, itself a National Nature Reserve.

All of which is excellent news for walkers! The walks presented here offer a range of possibilities: a tough trek along the exposed north coast cliffs to Crackington Haven – past a rare patch of ancient Western oak woodland – visiting the remote church at St Gennys, once site of a holy well; an exploration of the serpentine rocks of Lizard Point, the southernmost point on the British mainland, where the red-legged Cornish chough is now breeding successfully after an absence of 50 years; or a pleasant wander along the peaceful Fowey Estuary to the ancient church at Lanteglos, where the novelist Daphne du Maurier was married in 1932.

Hawker Country

Start

Morwenstow, north of Bude

Distance

4¾ miles (7.6km)

Height gain

1,475 feet (450m)

Approximate time

3 hours

Route terrain

Rolling farmland and strenuous Coast Path: steep ascents and descents

P Parking

Parking area at Morwenstow church: Morwenstow is 11½ miles (18.4km) north of Bude via A39

Dog friendly

To be kept on leads through fields; some non-dog-friendly stiles and possibility of geese at Yeolmouth

OS maps

Landranger 190 (Bude & Clovelly),Explorer 126 (Clovelly & Hartland)

GPS waypoints

   SS 206 152
Ⓐ SS 215 166
Ⓑ SS 217 171
Ⓒ SS 212 173
Ⓓ SS 212 174
Ⓔ SS 199 152

On the map this looks a short walk so that the time taken seems surprising. Perhaps it is explained by the fascinating church at the start, and by the lonely, savage beauty of Marsland Mouth, where Devon meets Cornwall and it is hard not to linger. If you have a dog with you look out for guard geese on some farms. There is strenuous climbing on this route.

There can be few churches that have a more dramatic location than the one at Morwenstow. Situated on the edge of a small valley that tumbles to the sea within ½ mile (800m), it is inevitable that the church should have strong maritime connections. Many a dead sailor lies buried in the churchyard – the famous white figurehead (removed for repair in 1989) came from the *Caledonia*, a Scottish brig which was wrecked off Morwenstow in 1842. Only one of her crew of ten seamen survived, the captain being buried beneath the site of the figurehead (on the left of the church path, just below the lychgate), while the rest of the crew, along with many other victims of the sea, are buried by the 'Upper Trees' where a tall granite cross bearing the words 'Unknown yet Well Known' marks the site of the communal grave.

This information comes from the peerless guide to the church which is crammed full of facts about the lovely building and its famous vicar from 1834, Robert Stephen Hawker. He is credited with being the inventor of the harvest festival – the first took place at Morwenstow in 1843, a celebration for good crops after years of famine – though he is better known for his literary work and philanthropy.

Our walk starts at the lychgate: turn right downhill through the churchyard to a stone stile to the right of Hawker's vicarage, now a private house. The curious chimneys of the building are said to represent the towers of various churches with which Hawker was associated, and that of his Oxford college. The path descends through trees to a footbridge and stile at the bottom of the valley, and then climbs the other side equally steeply. Keep straight on at a footpath junction to reach the top. Pass through a gate and continue with the hedge on the right. Keep straight on, passing the farm right, following signs for the alternative path avoiding farmyard. Cross the ladder stile over the next hedge, and turn right. Turn right through the next gateway, and bear left to meet a concrete road. Immediately follow footpath signs left through a gate.

Keep the hedge on the left and eventually cross a stile at Yeolmouth. Keep ahead to pass a small barn, and bear right through a gate onto a track. Bear left when this meets with a made-up road, descending towards Cornakey Farm. Turn right on the alternative path before reaching the farmyard; walk through the field, then turn left onto a track through a small gate. Turn right. Pass a gate on the left and keep on to the gate at the end of the enclosed track; keep ahead, with a hedge on the right, to pass through another gate. Bear left and cross the field diagonally to a triple stile.

Bear slightly left across the next field, towards woods at the bottom, heading for the buildings beyond the trees. Cross a stile and climb down a very steep bank, with rough steps, to two

footbridges Ⓐ at the bottom. On the opposite side of the valley the path uses part of an ancient track. At the top of the hill follow the alternative permissive path right to pass Marsland Manor (left). Follow signs briefly right then left to reach a stile onto the lane, where you turn left.

At the junction take the 'Unsuitable for Motors' lane signposted to Marsland Mouth. Pass through the gate and bear to the left when the paths divide Ⓑ.

SCALE 1:25 000 or 2½ INCHES to 1 MILE 4CM to 1KM

Church of St Morwenna and John the Baptist, Morwenstow

Pass through another gate and keep right at a fork, then bear right **C** to descend to sea level. It's well worth the effort, especially if there's a good sea running (and there usually is). The Mouth is a wonderful wild place, often utterly deserted – the loneliness is exhilarating. If you cross the stream **D** you are in Devon, and you have to do this to reach the beach – an excellent place to picnic.

Climb back from the beach, cross the bridge back into Cornwall, and take the Coast Path on the right **C**. Of course it is a steep climb, but the views back are rewarding. Note the contorted strata of Gull Rock below and the fine view inland. There is a seat at the top so you can regain breath and enjoy the view before the descent to Litter Mouth, which is helped by good steps; the

zigzag climb on the other side, partially stepped, is a hard 15-minute slog to a kissing-gate.

Follow the cliff edge down to Yeol Mouth, then climb again. Then there is a short stretch of level ground along Henna Cliff before the descent to Morwenstow begins. The sinister radar dishes at Coombe are now in view ahead. The final up-and-down comes at Morwenstow itself, the climb up to Vicarage (or Rectory) Cliff being made up for by the superb view to the south-west, the inspiration for many of Hawker's verses. This is coastal scenery at its most awesome. Turn left **E** inside the gate at the top of the cliffs to return to Morwenstow church and refreshment at **Rectory Farm Tea Rooms** (seasonal) opposite.

Dizzard Point

There can be few more energetic sections of the Coast Path than this, and few that are less trodden. But the walking here is exhilarating, and the steep climbs all seem worth while when a pause is made to take in the view. Only a very short part of the walk uses a road carrying much traffic, and the final section passes through a rare example of Cornwall's primeval woodland.

As you drive south-west from Millook keep a watch for a cottage on the right called Cancleave. The parking spaces are on the other side of the road. Use the stile on the seaward side of the road opposite the parking area to reach a path which joins the coastal footpath within a few yards. Turn left here, but first look back towards Millook to see an example of the geological folding for which this area is famous.

Unusually, the path follows the edge of the cliff on unworn grass. It skirts the side of a wooded combe before plunging into it. A stile drops to a stream crossing, and then the path climbs steeply to reach Bynorth Cliff. Follow the right edge of the field, eventually enjoying a fine view back across Widemouth Bay. The trees on the cliffs here are mainly stunted oaks, well beaten by the gales: this is a tough walk in a strong westerly. Cross three stiles to pass a triangulation pillar above Dizzard Point with a spot-height of 538 feet (164m). Go through two kissing-gates. At the end of the next field bear right to a kissing-gate that leads the path to the cliff edge. The view to the east is even better. The cliff-edge vegetation is now of stunted oaks with a few examples of gorse, which always seems to be able to show a flower even in the bleakest months.

The first great test of stamina is now to be faced. At Chipman Point **A** the path plunges down a precipitous cliff-face (up to now the cliffs, though high, have been gently-sloping). Note the contorted strata far below, and the daunting climb up the opposite side of this valley. Fortunately steps (though big and difficult) negotiate much of the descent and ascent. Note the waterfall above the beach and, at the top of the combe, the tower of St Gennys Church ahead. The Coast Path hugs the cliff and reaches another (less severe) descent and ascent, crossing a stream via a bridge. Nearby on the left can be seen the farmhouse of Cleave and the scant remains of the medieval village of Tresmorn.

Eventually cross a stile and follow the Coast Path out on to the headland of Castle Point – this is quite exposed in places –

walk 10

Start
Cancleave near Millook, south-west of Bude

Distance
8¼ miles (13.2km)

Height gain
1,690 feet (515m)

Approximate time
4½ hours

Route terrain
Very strenuous Coast Path; undulating return via fields and woodland

Parking
Parking space for Cancleave Strand, 1 mile (1.6km) south-west of Millook, south of Bude

Dog friendly
To be kept on leads through fields; some non-dog-friendly stiles

OS maps
Landranger 190 (Bude & Clovelly), Explorer 111 (Bude, Boscastle & Tintagel)

GPS waypoints
SX 175 992
A SX 158 987
B SX 142 972
C SX 162 969
D SX 169 980

before dropping down to the valley. This is National Trust land. The steep climb up the other side of the valley is aided by steps in places. Walk on to pass through two kissing-gates to reach a Coast Path post **B** at the landward end of Pencannow Point, the final headland before Crackington Haven is reached. It is possible to glimpse Tintagel from here, beyond Cambeak which guards the entrance to Crackington Haven. *If you need refreshment follow the Coast Path down to the village from here, but note that the climb back would be severe. Study of the map will show less arduous ways of regaining the route, though probably at the expense of missing St Gennys.*

If you do not want to go to the village, keep to the route by turning left and following the fence inland to reach a kissing-gate. Now a traditional Cornish hedgebank is on the left, and this accompanies the path to the hamlet of St Gennys. Follow the field edge, which bears right and then left to reach a kissing-gate. Pass through and descend to the church, which provides a perfect foreground to a panorama of

St Gennys

farmland and coastline. The church is a quiet and beautiful place to rest. St Genny was St Genesius, who according to tradition was beheaded and walked about with his head beneath his arm.

On leaving the church turn left and take the road past the Old School House, following it to the main Crackington road *(where those who sought refreshment would probably rejoin the route)*. Turn left to continue to a junction by an abandoned Methodist church, and turn left to Coxford. At the bottom of the steep hill **C**, just before Coxford Cottage, cross the footbridge on the left. Pick your way up through a group of trees then head up the steepest part of the field, bearing left to find a stile between two gates. Keep the hedge on the right after this, still climbing, though less strenuously now. There are fine views from here over the countryside covered earlier. The path reaches an enclosed lane which leads to the road coming from Tresmorn; turn right on to this.

When this byway reaches the lane to Millook turn left, and follow it for about ¼ mile (400m) to a white bungalow (Glencove) on the right, by the drive to Trengayor **D**. Turn right along the drive and through the farmyard; pass to the left of a cream house and through a gate onto a track, soon passing through another gate. Just before the next metal gate across this, turn left on the marked footpath

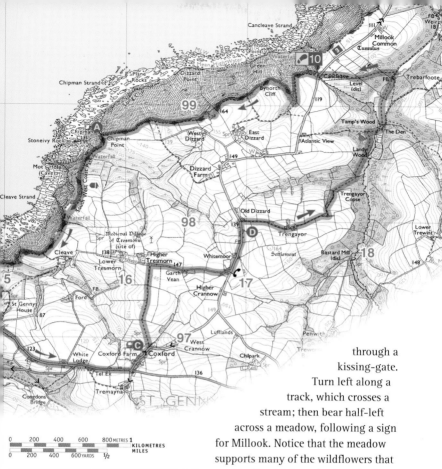

Scale bar:
```
0    200   400   600   800 METRES 1
                                  KILOMETRES
                                  MILES
0    200   400   600 YARDS  ½
```

through a wooden gate bearing a Woodland Trust logo (Millook Valley). Take the path to enter one of Cornwall's finest and most atmospheric primeval woods. The abundance of small woodland bird species emphasises the value of this sort of natural environment. The trees are mainly tall, thin oaks, often adorned with tree ferns, but there are many other indigenous species, most notably holly. The footpath descends steadily; at the bottom go down steps to cross the stream.

The path follows the left bank of the stream. Eventually a white house appears through the trees to the right; turn right to cross the footbridge over the stream, and then the meadow beyond to pass behind a house and through a kissing-gate. Turn left along a track, which crosses a stream; then bear half-left across a meadow, following a sign for Millook. Notice that the meadow supports many of the wildflowers that used to flourish in such places before the widespread use of fertilisers. At the end of the meadow re-enter the wood. The stream (Millook Water) is now on the left.

The next landmark to be seen is the charming cottage at Trebarfoote Coombe, thatched until a fire destroyed its roof. Cross the footbridge before reaching it onto a track; 20 yards later turn left uphill on a narrow woodland path signed Cancleave. Eventually a gate is reached, and after this continue to follow the left side of the valley to a stile. This is a good point at which to pause and look back at the countryside. Follow the path steeply uphill along the edge of fields, eventually crossing a stile to reach the road to the right of the parking place at Cancleave. ●

Tintagel & Boscastle

Start
Tintagel

Distance
10 miles (16km)

Height gain
1,920 feet (585m)

Approximate time
5½ hours

Route terrain
Undulating Coast Path, rocky in places; rolling farmland and wooded river valley, uneven underfoot at times

Parking
Car parks (fee-paying) off Tintagel's main street

Dog friendly
To be kept on leads through fields; some non-dog-friendly stiles

OS maps
Landrangers 190 (Bude & Clovelly) and 200 (Newquay & Bodmin), Explorer 111 (Bude, Boscastle & Tintagel)

GPS waypoints
SX 056 884
Ⓐ SX 052 890
Ⓑ SX 062 896
Ⓒ SX 072 895
Ⓓ SX 077 906
Ⓔ SX 091 909
Ⓕ SX 096 904
Ⓖ SX 092 889
Ⓗ SX 081 885

The outward section of this walk uses a particularly spectacular stretch of the coastal footpath, and the walk would be worth doing for that alone; but we also have a lovely section through fields and the richly wooded St Nectan's Glen, with its waterfall. As a bonus there is the opportunity of exploring a most beautiful fishing village. This is a strenuous walk, but very rewarding.

The Old Post Office stands on the south-western side of Tintagel's main street. Keep it on your left and walk ahead; where the road bears right towards the Castle Car Park turn left at a sign 'To the Coast Path'. The path to the castle descends steeply, parallel to and then along a lane (there is a Land Rover service available for visitors not able to take exercise).

Walking down the main street of Tintagel one is almost overwhelmed by the gift shops selling souvenirs celebrating the Arthurian legend and left with a sense of foreboding that the castle and coastline will prove to be something of a let-down. However, few visitors will fail to recognise the romance of the place, which is perhaps best appreciated at a distance – away from the crowds.

Our route follows the Coast Path, which bears to the right away from the castle below **Tintagel Castle Beach Café Ⓐ**, and quite soon the throngs thin out and one can sit and contemplate the great headland made famous by the inspiration of Tennyson. Even if you have earlier paid your money to English Heritage to visit the castle (the ruins you see are of a castle built in the 13th century – nothing remains of Arthur's stronghold, if there ever was one) it is best to savour the place from near the opposing headland, Barras Nose. This is famous for its gloomy cave, well seen from the Coast Path. It was one of the National Trust's first properties, having been acquired in 1896.

Follow the Coast Path past Barras Nose. The next headland is even more memorable: Willapark Ⓑ, not to be confused with another Willapark that overlooks Boscastle harbour. As the path drops to Bossiney one cannot avoid noticing the ranks of caravans drawn up on the cliff top, both on the right and ahead. The descent to Bossiney can be difficult if wet, though there are steps on the other side to help with the climb.

The view ahead is now of a succession of magnificent headlands, with seas beating against their precipitous flanks and pouring off rocky ledges. The sound is as marvellous as the sight: think of the terrible plight of those wrecked off this shore in days gone by. Pause before the descent to Rocky Valley to notice how the scenery becomes even more rugged beyond, especially with the jagged spires of rock off Trevalga Cliff.

Rocky Valley itself **C** is delightful, fully living up to its name. Small waterfalls and swirlholes interrupt the sparkling progress of the little stream, which flows through a narrow glen-like valley (appropriately, for this is the seaward end of St Nectan's Glen). The climb back up to the clifftop is quite severe.

Ladies Window

Firebeacon Hill is notable for a pinnacle of rock on its western side and for the remarkable formation known as the Ladies Window which is best seen from a rocky outcrop to the left of the path at the top **D**.

After yet another descent and ascent at Welltown, the path approaches the next great headland – Willapark, which has a murky zawn (a sea cave aptly named Western Blackapit) at its base. Here **E** there is a choice of routes. *If you are already familiar with Boscastle and wish to avoid the steep climb out of the village, turn right here to pass through the Farraday Stitches – an area of ancient strip cultivation – aiming for the church and Paradise (see map).*

The more usual way will be to visit the picturesque little village of Boscastle. You can either keep on the Coast Path as it rounds the cliff above the quay, or take the left fork down to the quay itself – *but take care – this path can be slippery*. Having explored the village's attractions, cross the main road to the lane (Old Road) by the **Wellington Hotel** and climb up steeply, bending left as it becomes Dunn St; continue steeply uphill and cross the main road to reach Paradise, a lovely street of old houses including the famous **Napoleon Inn**, which dates from the 16th century; a century or so ago, when the fortunes of the harbour were at their zenith, the village had 18 alehouses. Turn right at the crossroads into Paradise Road; where this level lane turns right to join the main road, take the lane on the left signed Trerosewill Farm **F**.

Keep straight on past the farmhouse;

after a Z-bend look for a stone stile on the right and cross two fields; there is a fine view of the village from here. Make for a triple stile and boardwalk in the top corner of the second field. Initially keep on the left side of the next field, following the waymark in the gap in the hedgebank ahead to cut across to a gate.

Pass through and turn left to stone steps and a stile. Bear right to a footpath post, then left to cross a stile in a wire fence. Continue uphill in the same direction to a gate in the top right-hand corner. Bear left along a green lane and follow it to a gate onto the road, where you turn right. Just after the driveway to Trehane Farm turn left into a farm track and look immediately for a stone stile on the right. Cross the field diagonally to a gate and stile at the bottom-right corner, to the right of the farm buildings, and turn left into a lane.

The lane winds down past Tredole Farm almost to the bottom of the valley, but just before you cross the stream turn right over a footpath-signed stile in the hedge **G**. Climb this to cross two narrow fields. At the far side of the second field there is a stile/footbridge/stile to cross. Keep the fence on the left and cross the stream left by the ford by another

footbridge. The path follows the left bank of the stream through the next meadow to a stile where the path divides.

Cross the stile and stream again to follow its right bank (muddy after wet weather). Where a ruined barn appears, the official path runs right uphill to cross a stile, then turns left downhill to reach the barn; this route may be hard to follow in summer. Continue along the right bank through fields and over stiles, eventually crossing a stile into the wooded glen itself. The path passes the **Hermitage Tea Garden** **H**, through which the waterfall can be accessed (entrance fee).

Continue along the right bank (the path is rocky in places). The path crosses over the stream twice, first by way of a wooden footbridge, then via a concrete one. At the third footbridge, turn left to cross it and follow the path to Halgabron up the side of the valley. Pass out of the glen at the top through

a kissing-gate. Go straight across the meadow to reach a wooden and a stone stile in the top left corner. Turn left into a lane; ignore the first footpath right, and take the second one right, which crosses a stone stile and then crosses a field. When you meet the far hedge keep it on the right, to reach a stone stile between houses. Keep ahead to meet the road.

Turn to the right down the road (*take care, especially in summer*) and when it bends to the right take the footpath signposted on the left, crossing the field diagonally to a stone stile in the bottom hedge. Maintain the same course over the next field to find a gate in the hedgebank. Cross the next field diagonally,

aiming for a stone stile to the left of a tall hedge; cross a wooden stile in a fence, then a stone stile to the right of the whitewashed house.

Turn left along the road which leads to the centre of Tintagel and the starting point.

TINTAGEL & BOSCASTLE ● **41**

walk 12

Start
Trevone Bay, west of Padstow

Distance
7¼ miles (11.5km)

Height gain
740 feet (225m)

Approximate time
3½ hours

Route terrain
Moderate Coast Path (one very steep short ascent); fields and farm tracks

P Parking
Car parks (fee-paying) at Trevone Bay; signed off B3276 west of Padstow

Dog friendly
To be kept on leads through fields

OS maps
Landranger 200 (Newquay & Bodmin), Explorer 106 (Newquay & Padstow)

GPS waypoints
- SW 892 759
- Ⓐ SW 890 763
- Ⓑ SW 910 784
- Ⓒ SW 921 761
- Ⓓ SW 914 757

Stepper Point from Trevone

This pleasant, fairly energetic walk covers a variety of coastal scenery with a contrasting inland section crossing the peninsula. The cliffs are exposed and lofty – be very careful if it is windy.

The car parks are on the north-eastern side of Trevone Bay below the **Madrips Café**. Take the coastal path which climbs to the clifftop, with the remarkable Round Hole Ⓐ on the right. If the weather is rough flecks of foam at the bottom show that there is a passage to the sea. It is a fascinating landform, illustrating how the sea exploits weaknesses in geological strata. There are excellent views westwards from Roundhole Point and farther on at Porthmissen there is another phenomenon – a rock bridge.

Note the contortions of the strata in the cliffs here; there are good views westwards to Trevose Head. The walking is delightful with springy turf underfoot. Ahead is a spectacular rock pinnacle; note too the fine view back. A steep climb leads to the cliffs above the pinnacle. Gulland Rock is offshore to the left, and as the path nears Gunver Head another deadly group of rocks known as King Phillip appears ahead off Pentire Head. The tower on Stepper Point comes into view.

At the Butter Hole the slaty rock is a wonderful deep blue to purple, with a sandy beach far below. The awful inevitability of shipwreck for a sailing ship embayed by an onshore wind must have inspired many a prayer here.

The Pepperpot on Stepper Point Ⓑ, also known as the Daymark, is dangerous to explore. The coastal footpath goes down here, though you can bear right before the Pepperpot on an alternative upper path which involves less climbing and passes in front of the coastguard lookout.

The path now follows the shore of the estuary, where the tide flows very fast and the Doom Bar was aptly named; certainly the sound of the surf here can be quite frightening.

Follow the lane round the back of Hawker's Cove, then over a stile to pass behind the old lifeboat station. At the next inlet (Harbour Cove) follow Coast Path signs inland, crossing a track, then duckboards. On meeting another track turn right, then left on the Coast Path along the edge of fields inside a band of sand dunes. It is possible to cut across the inlet by crossing the stream and sands, *but be warned that the tide comes in quickly.* The Coast Path can be regained by walking through the dunes on the other side of the cove. After this cove the view of the River Camel ahead is stunning – the Rock ferry can be seen in the distance. If the tide is out the walk along the beach, rather than on the low cliffs, is a pleasant change. St George's Cove is an inviting place for a picnic or a paddle, though dogs are forbidden.

Our path turns off to the right before the iron gates leading to the War Memorial **C**, but it is worth taking the extra few steps for the memorable view. *Should you wish to visit Padstow keep on the coast path.* To rejoin the route take the first right turning from North Quay, and then right again, passing the Post Office on your right. Take the right fork, pass Prideaux Place, and go under the bridge.

Climb up on the edge of the fields with the hedge on the left. This is a pleasant field walk, giving occasional glimpses of Padstow and its river. It soon reaches the perimeter wall of the Prideaux Place Deer Park. Turn right on to the lane **D** and where this becomes level, after about 500 yards, there is a footpath sign and steps on the left. Climb these and cross the

field diagonally. Cross a track and then a stone stile into another field which is also crossed diagonally. Cross straight over the next small field and the following one diagonally, noticing the lovely view. Head for the buildings over the next field. There are now two more fields to cross before reaching a track which leads left to the settlement of Crugmeer.

Turn to the right for a very short distance before taking a lane on the left leading towards some old buildings. Pass by these and continue along the lane which passes in front of Porthmissen Farm. It then drops steeply to reach the car parks at Trevone Bay.

SCALE 1:29412 or 2¼ INCHES to 1 MILE 3.4CM to 1KM

walk 13

Porthcurno & Porthgwarra

Start

Porthcurno

Distance

5 miles (7.9km)

Height gain

835 feet (255m)

Approximate time

2½ hours

Route terrain

Undulating Coast Path, fields and farm tracks

Parking

Porthcurno beach car park (fee-paying); Porthcurno 3½ miles (5.6km) south-east of Land's End, signed off B3315

Dog friendly

To be kept on leads through fields; some non-dog-friendly stiles

OS maps

Landranger 203 (Land's End & Isles of Scilly), Explorer 102 (Land's End)

GPS waypoints

SW 385 225
Ⓐ SW 384 217
Ⓑ SW 372 217
Ⓒ SW 364 226
Ⓓ SW 373 228

This lovely walk explores the cliffs to the west of popular Porthcurno, some of the most magnificent in West Penwith. The tiny hamlet of Porthgwarra ('higher cove' in Cornish) – more accessible by foot than car – is soon reached, a cluster of cottages and small beach with a forgotten feel (and refreshments in season). Heather and Western gorse – beautiful in August – carpet Ardensawah Cliff, with opportunities to linger and soak up the scenery. Narrow paths weave inland, before easy field paths lead to medieval St Levan's Church, extended in the 15th century.

Leave the lower car park and take the path to the beach. On reaching the Coast Path turn right. *En route to the beach a path right leads to the* **Porthcurno Beach Café** *and road; those wishing for a less strenuous route to the clifftop should turn right here, then left on meeting the road, which is then followed uphill to rejoin the route in the Minack Theatre car park.* The Coast Path runs along the western side of the beach, with wonderful views towards Logan Rock, before threading its way steeply up the cliffs which provide a romantic backdrop for the Minack Theatre and **café**.

The steep climb ends at the theatre's car park; cross this to find the Coast Path on the far side. This leads to the spectacular headland of Pedn-mên-an-mere Ⓐ, though the National Trust prefers to call this property Rospletha Cliffs. The gradual descent to Porth Chapel is in contrast to the steep climb up the other side of the cove, passing St Levan's holy well en route; the tower of St Levan's Church can be clearly seen to landward after the ascent. Turn left along the Coast Path to reach Carn Barges with more dramatic scenery, before descending to Porthgwarra Ⓑ. Note the perched rock on the left and the landmarks on the hill ahead.

As you climb the coastal path from Porthgwarra you will probably hear the sound of the Runnel Stone buoy, ¾ mile (1.2km) out to sea. After Hella Point the jagged rocks around Polostoc Zawn and Gwennap Head remind us how perilous this coastline was in the days of sail. Land's End can now be clearly seen in the distance. The reddish colour of the intricately jointed rocks of the cliffs contrasts with the green hue of those at the top covered with lichen. A maze of footpaths wanders across Carn Guthenbrâs: the narrow path hugging the clifftops

SCALE 1:27 777 or 2¼ INCHES to 1 MILE 3.6CM to 1KM

leads to a narrow arrête between a blowhole and sheer cliffs, *so take care. Unless you have a good head for heights and are extremely sure-footed, it's best to aim for the National Coastwatch Station on Gwennap Head.* The path drops to Porth Loe, then ascends steeply. Follow it on to pass through a stone wall, then turn right and follow the wall inland. Turn left, then bear right along a path through heather and gorse, aiming to the right of the tower of Sennen church.

Turn right at a footpath junction **C** towards a cream-coloured house on the skyline; there is a ruined cottage to the left. The path threads through the gorse to meet a track coming from Arden-Sawah: this is a bridleway. Pass to the right of the cream house; at the entrance to the farmyard at Arden-Sawah turn left on to a concrete driveway to meet the lane going to Porthgwarra, then turn right.

Ignore the first footpath left, and take the second footpath to the left over a stile **D**, from where you will see the tower of St Levan's Church. Follow the path down with the hedge on the right.

Cross the stile ahead to continue on the same course but now with the hedge on the left. The fields here are very small, sometimes only 3–4 acres (1.2–1.6ha).

Carry straight on over another stile (these were designed to be crossed without losing one's stride). A series of stiles follows along the path; eventually bear left over a stile, and follow the field edge, to cross a stile to the right of cottages by St Levan's Church. This has the dignified simplicity characteristic of medieval Cornish churches; in the churchyard is the split rock which is said to have been St Levan's favourite place of repose. He prophesied that if a donkey should ever be driven through the cleft the world would end.

Pass up steps into the churchyard; leave the churchyard over a stile by the ancient cross at its eastern (left) end. Cross the stile and gate at the top of the field and follow the path over the next field past the remains of another ancient cross. The path leads to the renovated farm buildings at Rospletha; turn right onto the lane to meet the road. The Minack Theatre is to the right; turn left down-hill to return to the starting point. ●

Lizard Point

Start

Lizard Point

Distance

7¾ miles (12.5km)

Height gain

1,035 feet (315m)

Approximate time

4 hours

Route terrain

Moderate Coast Path but lengthy; tracks across Lizard Downs, muddy after wet weather

Parking

NT car park by lighthouse

Dog friendly

On leads through National Nature Reserve

OS maps

Landrangers 203 (Land's End & Isles of Scilly) and 204 (Truro & Falmouth), Explorer 103 (The Lizard)

GPS waypoints

  SW 702 116
Ⓐ SW 696 115
Ⓑ SW 684 133
Ⓒ SW 700 145
Ⓓ SW 712 143
Ⓔ SW 720 143
Ⓕ SW 715 119

It looks quite a short distance on the map but this is deceptive, as the Coast Path is exceptionally tortuous, though without severe gradients. The scenery is outstanding, especially if a rough sea is running, and the inland leg makes a pleasant contrast with the coastal sections.

From the lower end of the car park (by the toilets) follow a path down to meet the coastal footpath, and turn right to reach Lizard Point, the most southerly tip of mainland Britain. Cross the access road and follow the Coast Path past the **Wavecrest Café**. From the first headland Ⓐ there is a fine view back to the squat lighthouse and the point. The colouring of the rocks of the Lizard is very distinctive; they lack the pinkish hue of those of the Land's End peninsula. They have evocative names such as Man of War, Barges Rock, the Stags and Shag Rock. All have played their part in claiming lives, and 207 were drowned when the *Royal Anne* was wrecked on the Stags in November, 1720. The victims were buried on the clifftop in Pistol Meadow, Polpeor.

Shipwreck occasionally had its lighter moments. When about 50 years later a Quebec-registered ship sailing for Hull hit the same reef the crew were able to scramble on to Crenvil Rock. The light of dawn showed one man clutching a large cask, and another desperately holding on to a live pig. When the crew staggered ashore they were met by the ship's cat which had also survived at the cost of half of its tail. They made a strange procession as they marched into the village, where they were able to drink the nine gallons of rum that the cask contained, and trade the pig for the price of a ride to Falmouth. The ginger cat was presented to the landlord of the inn, where it led a contented life until it died of old age.

From Old Lizard Head the view ahead opens up with the shapes of the rock stacks of Kynance in the distance ahead. The crowds will now have thinned out and there is springy level turf to walk on between a run of descents and ascents, with a number of Cornish stiles en route. Almost too soon the National Trust's car park for Kynance Cove comes into view. The Trust has an excellent leaflet on the history, human and natural, of the cove. This was one of the places beloved by the 'Excursionists' of the 19th century. Prince Albert brought his

Lizard Point

children ashore here in 1846, and Tennyson paid his first visit to the cove two years later. It was the Victorians who were responsible for giving the various features of the area such fanciful names – where did the inspiration for Asparagus Island come from?

Follow the path past the car park to join a gritty path, then rough steps leading down into the valley. Turn left to reach the cove. (*Note: at times of exceptionally high tide there is an alternative coast path route signed right as you descend towards the cove.*) Drop down steps, then cross rocky ground at the back of the cove; turn right immediately past the **café** Ⓑ and follow

the rough track as it zigzags up the cliffs. Where this levels off and bears right, fork left along a broad, stony bridlepath which strikes in a fairly straight line across the heath, paralleling the valley to the left. The heather, *Erica vagans*, is unique to this small part of Britain.

Head for a row of houses which comes into view in the distance. The heath – Lizard Downs – is part of the Lizard NNR. This area has been dug over in the past for the raw material for serpentine working; there are lots of tracks and small ponds harbouring wildlife. Much of the path can be muddy.

The bridlepath passes through a gate,

and then meets the road. Cross over by the petrol station **C** to a track on the opposite side (at the left end of the row of houses mentioned earlier). This track soon opens into a lovely heathy wilderness with the tower of St Grade's Church in sight ahead (more correctly, St Grada of the Holy Cross). Another stretch of enclosed gritty path leads to the road.

Turn right and keep straight on at the junction, heading for Grade. Take the track on the left to the church **D** – a place of tranquillity. There is no electric power here and for services the church is lit by oil lamps and the organ bellows pumped by hand.

Leave the churchyard at the eastern end over two stiles. Keep the hedgebank on the left. Ignore the path junction in the bottom left-hand corner, and keep going to the bottom right-hand corner of the field, where a stone stile and enclosed path lead to a gate into a field, and then the road. Cross the road, passing to the left of a white house. Follow the lane straight ahead towards Inglewidden. Follow the lane left at the next junction (private drive to White Heather ahead). Where the lane branches to the right **E** you can keep straight on along the Coast Path into Cadgwith (**Cadgwith Cove Inn** and **The Old Cellars café/restaurant**, then retrace your steps), but the route for the Lizard turns right following the sign for Inglewidden. Keep straight on past Townplace, a National Trust cottage, and over a stone stile to find the Devil's Frying Pan, a spectacular natural feature of a rock arch below sheer cliffs which curve like a basin around it. You are now on the coastal footpath again, heading south.

The subsequent going along the coastal path is straightforward, if energetic. Bass Point and the lifeboat

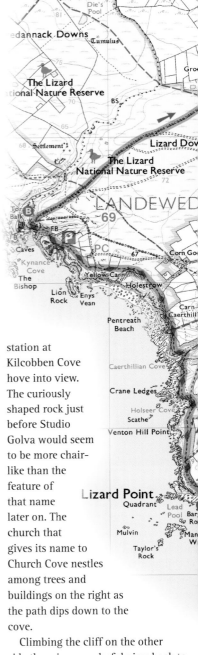

station at Kilcobben Cove hove into view. The curiously shaped rock just before Studio Golva would seem to be more chair-like than the feature of that name later on. The church that gives its name to Church Cove nestles among trees and buildings on the right as the path dips down to the cove.

Climbing the cliff on the other side there is a wonderful view back to Cadgwith and beyond. The path here crosses slopes carpeted with bluebells and white three-cornered leek in May – a beautiful sight. The path passes immediately behind the lifeboat station and in front of the coastguards' lookout

signalling apparatus this was of great importance as ships had to sail close in to the dangerous shore in order to send or receive vital signals (which were small squares of bunting hung from a mast). The Lizard Lighthouse comes into view ahead. Pen Olver is the rocky headland to the left as the path follows a stone hedge past an old bungalow. Guglielmo Marconi used the building for his pioneering work on wireless telegraphy.

Follow the Coast Path on to pass in front of the **Housel Bay Hotel**, then ascend the cliffs again and walk on the seaward side of the lighthouse, before turning right back to the car park. ●

on Bass Point ⓕ. Just beyond this is a white castellated building which was the Lloyd's Signal Station. Before the electric telegraph and efficient

walk 15

Polruan

Start
Polruan

Distance
5 miles (8.2km)

Height gain
1,050 feet (320m)

Approximate time
2½ hours

Route terrain
River valley woodland, lanes, moderate Coast Path

Parking
Polruan upper car park (fee-paying); follow signs from top of village

Dog friendly
Under control at all times

OS maps
Landrangers 200 (Newquay & Bodmin) and 201 (Plymouth & Launceston), Explorer 107 (St Austell & Liskeard)

GPS waypoints
SX 125 508
Ⓐ SX 127 510
Ⓑ SX 136 513
Ⓒ SX 144 517
Ⓓ SX 144 515
Ⓔ SX 149 510

Polruan is one of Cornwall's better-kept secrets, and this walk offers the chance to see its beautiful setting. Lanteglos church is also off the beaten track and deserves to be better known. This short walk has some quite severe, though not lengthy, gradients.

Leave the car park and turn right for a few yards. Turn left opposite the toilets and descend to the harbour by taking the winding footpath that runs downhill, bearing left; meet a lane (on the right) and keep left down Tinker's Hill, turning right when you reach the bottom. Instead of turning left to the quay follow the carved signpost straight on for the 'Hall Walk'. By now you will be aware of the wide choice of refreshments offered here in pubs and cafés.

The way at first follows a narrow lane – East Street – then at some steps turn right following 'The Hills' sign on a house. Climb the steps and turn left at the wooden sign 'Hall Walk'. Panoramic views of the river open up on the left Ⓐ as the path climbs steeply. Strategically placed seats give one a welcome place to recover and enjoy the view at the same time.

Keep to the upper path when it forks (20 yards on there is a National Trust sign 'North Downs'). The trees close in as the path turns to follow the creek below. When it meets a track Ⓑ (a signpost indicates backwards to Polruan) turn right and follow this for 20 yards before turning left through the trees, signed Pont & Bodinnick. Cross a small stream, and just past a bench continue along the path, ignoring another path right signed 'Lanteglos Church'. There are views towards the head of the creek below and a short steep climb to a gate on to the road. Do not go through – there is a National Trust sign 'Pont Pill' – keep on a footpath following a signpost 'Pont & Bodinnick' by bearing left and going through a gate.

The path follows the road down, but on the opposite side of the hedgebank. The field slopes steeply down towards the water; the path is steep, too, as it descends to the head of the creek. Go down steps and through a gate. Continue down more steps, bearing right as another footpath joins from the left, to reach the road again, and then turn left Ⓒ.

Almost immediately, at the corner by Little Churchtown Farm, turn right off the road, through a gate marked 'Footpath to the church', up a pleasant woodland track. This becomes quite a climb until a white gate appears ahead. Pass through this to reach the church of Lanteglos-by-Fowey .

The lovely church stands in this seemingly lonely position because it was built to serve Polruan and the four scattered hamlets of the peninsula: thus it is roughly central for all the district. It is dedicated to St Wyllow, a Christian hermit living in this part of Cornwall long before St Augustine and his followers landed in Kent in 597. He is believed to have been killed close to the head of the creek, a martyr to his faith. Fragments of a Norman church survive in the existing fabric, though most of what we see today dates from the 14th century. The church was fortunate in not being over-restored in the 19th century, although drastic repairs had to be made between 1896 and 1906.

From the porch leave the churchyard by the gate in the wall opposite, turning left down the lane. This soon climbs quite steeply to pass the National Trust's Pencarrow car park on the left before reaching the 'main' road. Go straight over and through the gate, then turn right to walk parallel to the road. Turn left through the next gate, crossing a field towards Pencarrow Head. Keep the hedge on your left.

At the next gate E *there is a choice: keep straight on if you wish to explore the headland and enjoy its views, or turn right before passing through the gate to take the coastal path back to Polruan.* This has very steep ups and downs but is enjoyable, both for the exercise it demands and for the scenery. The two Lantic beaches can be seen below and are accessible by a very steep path.

From Blackbottle Rock, another excellent viewpoint, the village is visible ahead, though this is deceptive as a fair walk is involved before you get there. Cross a stream and continue on the Coast Path; eventually it rises right to pass through a gate to the right of a white house. Turn left along the lane to regain the car park.

SCALE 1:27777 or 2¼ INCHES to 1 MILE 3.6CM to 1KM

SCALE

0   200   400   600   800 METRES   1
                                         KILOMETRES
                                         MILES
0   200   400   600 YARDS   ½

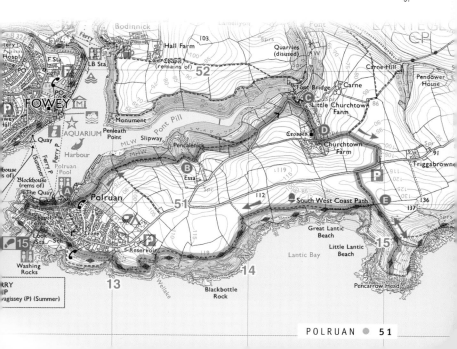

walk 16

Start

Entrance to Kilminorth Wood, West Looe

Distance

7½ miles (12km)

Height gain

1,000 feet (305m)

Approximate time

4 hours

Route terrain

Wooded riverside path, fields, undemanding Coast Path

P Parking

Millpool car park, West Looe (fee-paying), on A387

Dog friendly

To be kept on leads through fields; some non-dog-friendly stiles

OS maps

Landranger 201 (Plymouth & Launceston), Explorer 107 (St Austell & Liskeard)

GPS waypoints

  SX 248 537
Ⓐ SX 245 540
Ⓑ SX 233 545
Ⓒ SX 232 525
Ⓓ SX 230 517
Ⓔ SX 226 516

Looe & Talland Bay

The descriptive notices about plants and birds on the first section through Kilminorth Woods certainly add to the enjoyment of a lovely creekside walk. The view of Talland on the descent from Tencreek is unforgettable, with the ancient tower of the church a foreground to the sweep of the bay. The walk back to Looe along the coastal path is enjoyable and undemanding.

From the top of the car park, take the Riverside Walk along the side of the river (not the bridleway which follows higher up, which runs through Kilminorth Woods local nature reserve). After about ½ mile (800m), when the path drops to the shore Ⓐ, look for steps on the left which climb steeply to skirt the site of an old boatyard and cross the Giant's Hedge before dropping back to the river again.

The Hedge is an earthwork which runs from here to Lerryn, a distance of nearly 5 miles (8km). Tradition says that the Devil built it when he had nothing better to do, but it is rather more likely to have been a tribal defensive work.

A path on the right allows access onto the saltmarsh as the river narrows; this can be followed *at low tide only* to avoid the steep steps around the old boatyard.

Eventually the Riverside Walk reaches a picturesque group of houses, Watergate Ⓑ, turn left and make your way up the lane. A pleasant byway which is little used by traffic, this climbs steadily up through the wood by a stream. Halfway up the hill the bridleway through the upper woods meets it from the left.

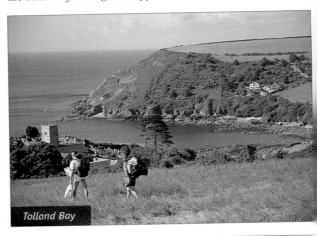

Tolland Bay

right **C** leads to
Tencreek Farm;
keep straight on,
looking for a waymarked
kissing-gate on the right to a
camping field. Keep the hedge
on the right and follow the yellow
waymark. Pass through a kissing-gate
on the right near the bottom of the
field; keep the hedge on the right and
walk round the edge of the field, aiming
for a point close to where electricity
cables cross over the hedge on the right.
There is a kissing-gate next to a metal
gate here, in the bottom corner of
the field.

The tower of Talland church can now

The wood ends before the large complex
of holiday homes on the right
(Kilminorth Farm Cottages) though the
lane continues its long climb. At last the
crest of the hill is reached and the view
looking back can be enjoyed.
Cross the main road and follow the lane
past Waylands Farm. A lane on the

be seen. Once through the gateway turn right, and follow the waymarked route around the edge of the field, keeping the hedge on the right. The path passes to the right of the Landmark, one of two showing a measured nautical mile to ships on speed trials at sea. The path passes over a stile and down steep steps to a lane **D**. Turn right down this to Talland church, worth visiting for its barrel roof and the carving on the bench ends. Note too the unusual, and sad, memorial to Joanna Mellow and her baby who died in childbirth in 1625. The carving on a slate slab in the floor at the east end of the church shows them both sitting up in a four-poster bed. The church has a covered way which serves as a porch and connects it to the detached tower.

From the church the lane descends steeply to Talland beach. There is a seasonal **café** here, and another straight along the lane on a sandy beach,

following Coast Path signs towards Polperro. At low tide the wreck of the French fishing trawler *Marguerite* can be seen in the bay.

Opposite the **Smugglers Rest café** and Smugglers Cottage – infamous for its involvement in drugs smuggling as late as 1980 – turn left **E** onto the Coast Path though a kissing-gate, then up a steep flight of wooden steps. Continue on the Coast Path to enter the National Trust's Hendersick property after about ½ mile (800m). The path changes direction opposite the jagged Hore Stone and Bridge Rocks. Now the view to the east can be seen, with St George's Island offshore and the houses of Hannafore Point on the far side of Portnadler Bay. The other landmark is visible on the hilltop to the west of Hannafore. There is a healthy population of cormorants (or maybe shags) inhabiting the rocks below.

The coastal path is very distinct and well used here. Lovely Samphire Beach is reached by a gate at its eastern end. It is a pleasant place for a picnic even though it is rather close to the crowds at Looe.

At Hannafore (look out for the ruins of Lammana Celtic chapel to the left) the route follows the pavement onto the West Looe waterfront, and then the road. Once parallel with the river there is an intermittent promenade along the riverside to keep walkers off the road. Go under the bridge, and turn right on hitting the lane to return to the car park and starting point.

Looe

17 *Yealm Estuary*

Tracks and undemanding Coast Path, partly along a carriage drive; estuary views

4½ miles (7.2km)

2½ hours

18 *Gara Rock & Portlemouth Down*

Tracks and fields, undemanding Coast Path

3½ miles (5.6km)

2 hours

19 *Prawle Point & Woodcombe Point*

Fields, tracks, undemanding Coast Path; short steep climb into village

5¾ miles (9.1km)

3 hours

20 *Start Point & Hallsands*

Coast Path, uneven underfoot in places, with steady final climb; quiet undulating lanes, some short ascents/descents

6½ miles (10.4km)

3½ hours

21 *Torcross & Slapton Ley*

Level Coast Path and around Slapton Ley; undulating lanes and fields, some steep and lengthy climbs

7 miles (11.2km)

3½ hours

Slapton Ley from Slapton Bridge

South Devon

The Coast Path in South Devon – which runs for around 100 miles (161km) from Devon's largest city, Plymouth, east to the Exe Estuary – is the most popular and softest part of the 630-mile (1,015-km) route. As a result the path, along with its gates, stiles and waymarking, tends to be better maintained and easier underfoot, and better serviced with refreshment stops and services, than elsewhere around the coast of the south-west peninsula. It is also the most popular part of Devon for both holidaymakers, and day-trippers – particularly during the summer months – from Plymouth and Torbay, the two largest centres of population in the county. And to further boost visitor figures the weather in this part of Devon – known as the South Hams – is frequently warmer and sunnier than, for example, over the inland heights of Dartmoor.

So walks in this area will tend to be busier than along the rest of the Coast Path, but will rarely be crowded – and the coastal scenery is unbelievably beautiful. The South Devon AONB holds much of the path – from the outskirts of Plymouth to Berry Head in Brixham, on the edge of Torbay – which is also a Heritage Coast, designated as a coastal preservation zone and containing many Sites of Special Scientific Interest. And despite the popularity of the area – inland a pastoral landscape of rolling green fields, deep-cut lanes and wooded valleys – on

Slapton Sands

Cottages at Newton Ferrers

your walks you will encounter sheltered and remote coves, such as those around Prawle Point, Devon's most southerly point, where the rocks date back some 400 million years; jagged headlands, such as Bolt Head near Salcombe and at Start Point; and peaceful, richly wooded river valleys such as the Dart and Yealm, an example of some of the finest ria coastline in Britain. Pretty thatched cottages and pubs lie tucked away in picturesque fishing ports such as Dartmouth and Salcombe, today popular with leisure sailors.

The walks suggested here stay away from the big coastal population centres and concentrate on the stunning stretch of coastline between the Yealm estuary and Torcross on Slapton Sands, a 3-mile (4.8km) long 3,000-year-old shingle barrier. Reed-fringed Slapton Ley, the largest natural lake in the Westcountry, which lies inside the barrier, is a National Nature Reserve on account of its birdlife. The wave-cut platforms and small, secluded sandy coves, often only accessible on foot, of Prawle Point are explored, with the opportunity of catching a ferry to Salcombe; and the beautiful wooded estuary of the Yealm is viewed from Lord Revelstoke's Drive, laid out in the 19th century by a local landowner for the benefit of his guests.

Slapton Ley

walk 17

Yealm Estuary

Start
Noss Mayo

Distance
4½ miles (7.2km)

Height gain
460 feet (140m)

Approximate time
2½ hours

Route terrain
Tracks and undemand-ing Coast Path, partly along a carriage drive; estuary views; initial steady ascent

P Parking
Car park at Noss Mayo; follow signs through village

Dog friendly
Under control at all times

OS maps
Landrangers 201 (Plymouth & Launceston) and 202 (Torbay & South Dartmoor), Explorer OL20 (South Devon)

GPS waypoints
SX 547 474
Ⓐ SX 541 466
Ⓑ SX 538 464
Ⓒ SX 547 475

A great advantage of this walk is that the only real climbing, a steady ¾ mile (1.2km) ascent, comes right at the beginning to reach the coast at The Warren. The rest of the route follows part of Revelstoke Drive, a flat and well-surfaced, 9-mile (14km) track laid out in the 19th century by Lord Revelstoke, a local landowner. The track follows an outstandingly attractive stretch of the coast before bearing right to continue along the beautiful, wooded shores of the Yealm estuary. On this final part of the walk there are superb views across the water to the houses of Newton Ferrers massed on the opposite shore.

Noss Mayo, situated on the south side of Newton Creek, an arm of the Yealm Estuary, is the twin village of Newton Ferrers on the north side. Both are extremely attractive and photogenic.

Start by turning left out of the car park, at a public footpath sign to 'The Warren', along an uphill lane. The lane continues as a rough track, ascending steadily all the while, and after ¾ mile (1.2km) it reaches a lane. Turn left and take the first turning on the right Ⓐ to pass through The Warren National Trust car park.

At the far end pass through a gate and bear right along a hedge-lined track towards the sea. Climb a stone stile and follow the track to the right and you will shortly pick up the Coast Path Ⓑ. Now comes a delightful stretch of coastal

Looking along the coast from Revelstoke Drive

walking along the well-constructed Revelstoke Drive, passing through several gates. The views ahead are most impressive looking towards the estuary of the River Yealm and beyond to Plymouth Sound. The track curves right to keep above the Yealm and later continues through attractive woodland fringing the estuary. On this section there are some gates and stiles, and at intervals gaps in the trees reveal fine views over the water.

The Yealm Estuary

Continue along a tarmac drive by the estuary and later beside Newton Creek into Noss Mayo. On the opposite side of the creek, the houses of Newton Ferrers, topped by the church tower, make a very attractive scene. Follow the lane to the right, passing in front of cottages. Continue uphill, passing the waterside **Ship Inn**, and at a junction turn right **C** along a lane with a 'No Through Road' sign to return to the start.

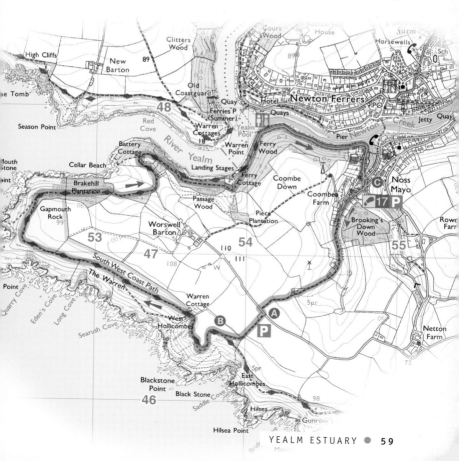

walk 18

Start

Mill Bay, follow signs from East Portlemouth. Alternatively it can be reached by ferry from Salcombe

Distance

3½ miles (5.6km)

Height gain

375 feet (115m)

Approximate time

2 hours

Route terrain

Tracks and fields, undemanding Coast Path

Parking

East Portlemouth: Mill Bay (NT) car park

Dog friendly

To be kept on leads through fields

OS maps

Landranger 202 (Torbay & South Dartmoor), Explorer OL20 (South Devon)

GPS waypoints

- SX 741 380
- Ⓐ SX 752 373
- Ⓑ SX 752 370

Gara Rock & Portlemouth Down

From the beach at Mill Bay, a steady uphill climb along a beautiful tree-lined track leads to the coast at the superb viewpoint of Gara Rock. The remainder of the route follows the Coast Path over Portlemouth Down and along the east side of the Salcombe estuary. Towards the end there are particularly fine views across the estuary to Salcombe.

At the beach turn left, at a public bridleway sign for Rickham, along a track that runs beside the car park. For the next ¾ mile (1.2km) follow this most attractive, shady track, lined by old pollarded lime trees, steadily climbing uphill to reach a wooden gate. Go through, cross a track, go up some steps and through a gate to continue uphill along an enclosed, sunken track.

Emerge from the trees, pass through a gate, and walk across the field, passing through a hedge gap. On the far side of the next field go through a gate onto a tarmac track Ⓐ. Turn right along it towards the coast; where it ends follow a low wall to the left, passing the new **Gara Rock** complex (refreshments). On the right here an unusual thatched lookout provides outstanding views along the coast, especially eastwards to Gammon Head. At the fingerpost turn right Ⓑ to join the Coast Path, in the direction of Mill Bay (signposted '2¼ miles').

Pass below the rock, descend steps and follow the winding and undulating coastal path back to the start. At first the view ahead is dominated by Bolt Head. Later the path curves right to continue along the side of the Salcombe estuary, with fine views across to Salcombe itself on the opposite side. Eventually the path passes above beaches, enters woodland and descends to Mill Bay.

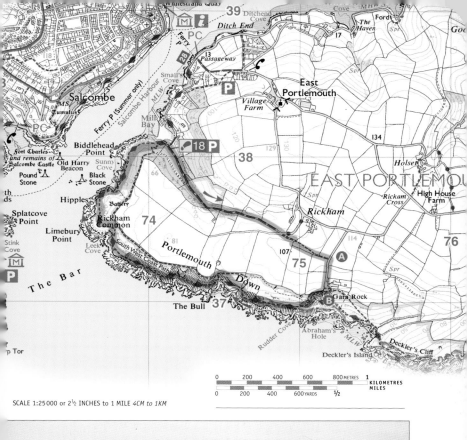

Looking eastwards from Gara Rock

Prawle Point & Woodcombe Point

Start

Prawle Point, just over one mile (1.6km) south of East Prawle

Distance

5¾ miles (9.1km)

Height gain

690 feet (210m)

Approximate time

3 hours

Route terrain

Fields, tracks, undemanding Coast Path; short steep climb into village

Parking

National Trust car park at Prawle Point

Dog friendly

To be kept on leads through fields; some non-dog-friendly stiles

OS maps

Landranger 202 (Torbay & South Dartmoor), Explorer OL20 (South Devon)

GPS waypoints

SX 774 354
Ⓐ SX 766 358
Ⓑ SX 767 361
Ⓒ SX 780 363
Ⓓ SX 786 371
Ⓔ SX 794 369

Prawle Point is the southern most tip of Devon and is situated amid some of the most dramatic coastal scenery in southern England. The walk starts by passing the Point and continuing along the coastline almost to Gammon Head. Then follows an inland section, mainly along enclosed paths and tracks, passing through the village of East Prawle and rejoining the coast at Woodcombe Sand. The final part of the route from Woodcombe Point to Prawle Point provides coastal walking at its finest.

Climb a stile by the car park entrance, walk downhill along the right-hand edge of a field to a fingerpost and turn right through a gate to join the Coast Path. Now comes a spectacular stretch of coastal walking: the path winds around this wild and rugged coastline, passing Prawle Point (call into the National Coastguard Watch visitor centre) and continuing around Elender Cove, with the jagged profile of Gammon Head visible ahead. There are several gates and stiles, but follow the yellow waymarks and acorn symbols all the time.

At a waymarked post above Maceley Cove turn right Ⓐ. Head up to the next waymarked post and turn left. Continue steadily uphill, go through a gate, and at a junction of paths and tracks turn right along an enclosed track Ⓑ. Keep along this to a lane. Follow the lane as it heads uphill and curves left into East Prawle.

In the village centre turn right Ⓒ in front of the **Pig's Nose Inn** and follow a lane to the left. Take the first turning on the right, continue along a curving lane heading uphill, and just in front of a telephone box turn right along a tarmac track. This later becomes a rough track, enclosed between high hedges, and passes the drive to Maelcombe House. Follow the track down into and out of a wooded area, then along the left edge of a field to a metal gate. Go through and turn right along a tarmac track Ⓓ, at a public bridleway sign to Lannacombe Green and Woodcombe Sand. Follow the track around a left bend and where the tarmac way bends right, keep ahead, at a public footpath/bridleway sign, along a grassy, enclosed track. At a fingerpost turn right, in the direction of Woodcombe Sand, to continue along a most

ttractive enclosed
ath. After going
hrough a gate, the
ath descends quite
teeply through
rees along the right
ide of a combe.
ollow the path as
: bends sharp left
nd drops to a
-junction of paths
bove Woodcombe
and.

Turn right **E** to rejoin the Coast Path,
nitially between bracken and bushes
elow Woodcombe Point. Start Point
an be seen to the left. Keep along the
Coast Path back to the start, negotiating
everal gates and following the regular

Gammon Head from Prawle Point

acorn symbol waymarks. In particular
look out for a sharp left turn, in the
Prawle Point direction, and follow the
field edge to the right to continue
towards Langerstone Point. Pass below
it and soon Prawle Point is seen. Keep
along the Coast Path as far as a
fingerpost in front of a gate, turn right,
on a public byway to East Prawle, and
retrace your steps to the car park.

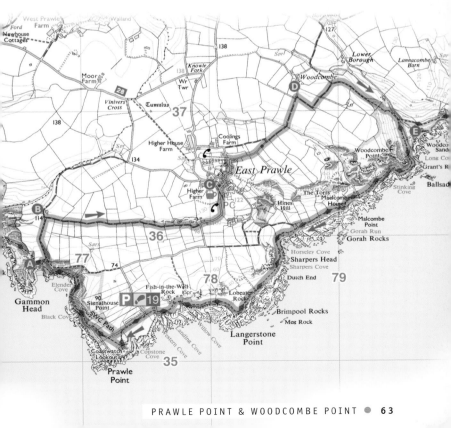

walk 20

Start

Car park at Start Point. Signposted from the A379 at Stokenham

Distance

6½ miles (10.4km)

Height gain

935 feet (285m)

Approximate time

3½ hours

Route terrain

Coast Path, uneven underfoot in places, with steady final climb; quiet undulating lanes, some short ascents/descents

P Parking

Car park at Start Point (fee-paying in season), 8 miles (13km) south-east of Kingsbridge

Dog friendly

Under control at all times

OS maps

Landranger 202 (Torbay & South Dartmoor), Explorer OL20 (South Devon)

GPS waypoints

🖉 SX 820 375
Ⓐ SX 824 372
Ⓑ SX 829 371
Ⓒ SX 802 372
Ⓓ SX 803 383
Ⓔ SX 817 385

Start Point & Hallsands

From the prominent headland of Start Point the views along the coast in both directions are outstanding and extensive: northwards across the wide expanse of Start Bay to Berry Head near Brixham, and westwards along one of the most spectacular stretches of the South Devon coast to Prawle Point and beyond to Bolt Head near Salcombe. After a short walk to Start Point, the route continues by heading westwards along the often rocky and dramatic Coast Path to Lannacombe Beach, and then turns inland through a steep-sided, wooded valley. An undulating section along lanes, steep in places, brings you back to the coast at the abandoned fishing village of Hallsands and the final stretch is a steady climb of nearly one mile (1.6km) above Start Bay. This is a superb walk but there are narrow paths in places and some fairly energetic climbs.

🖉 Begin by going through a white gate and walking along the tarmac lighthouse road to Start Point. At a fingerpost Ⓐ keep ahead along the road for a short detour to the lighthouse at the tip of Start Point Ⓑ to enjoy the magnificent views that encompass a large stretch of the South Devon coast.

Return to the fingerpost and turn left Ⓐ along the Coast Path which cuts across the narrow neck of the point. The path makes

Looking across Lannacombe Bay

initially for Frenchman's Rock, passing around the jagged pinnacles – *take care here, there are some sheer drops.* On the next part of the walk the views across Lannacombe Bay to Prawle Point are outstanding as you follow the winding and undulating path along this dramatic and rugged coast to reach Lannacombe Beach.

Go through a gate just before reaching the beach and turn right **C**, leaving the Coast Path, and continue along a narrow, tree- and hedge-lined track – later it becomes a tarmac track – for 1 mile (1.6km) through a thickly wooded and steep-sided valley.

At a T-junction, turn right **D** to continue along a lane which heads uphill to a crossroads at Hollowcombe Head. Keep ahead, in the South Hallsands direction, and the lane soon turns right and descends to the coast above the ruined fishing village of

Hallsands (which can be seen from the viewing platform – follow the signs). The village was abandoned after being destroyed during a violent storm in January 1917 and controversy has raged ever since over why this disaster was actually allowed to happen and was not avoided. One theory blames the sand dredging operations, which had been allowed since 1897, alleging that these had lowered the level of the beach, which used to protect the village. But over the centuries other villages on this stretch of coast have been similarly destroyed by the sea, so perhaps the catastrophe was inevitable.

Turn right **E** on to the Coast Path for a steady, continuous climb of 1 mile (1.6km) to return to the start, enjoying more fine views of Start Point and Start Bay. ●

Start

Torcross. Car park on north side of village

Distance

7 miles (11.2km)

Height gain

755 feet (230m)

Approximate time

3½ hours

Route terrain

Level Coast Path and around Slapton Ley; undulating lanes and fields, some steep and lengthy climbs

P Parking

Car park at Torcross (fee-paying), 6½ miles (10.5km) east of Kingsbridge

Dog friendly

To be kept on leads through fields; some non-dog-friendly stiles

OS maps

Landranger 202 (Torbay & South Dartmoor), Explorer OL20 (South Devon)

GPS waypoints

- SX 823 424
- Ⓐ SX 827 443
- Ⓑ SX 821 443
- Ⓒ SX 813 445
- Ⓓ SX 802 434
- Ⓔ SX 806 432
- Ⓕ SX 807 427
- Ⓖ SX 820 413

Torcross & Slapton Ley

There is a great variety of terrain and considerable historic interest on this walk. The scenic variety includes a walk beside the raised shingle beach of Slapton Sands, the lagoon and marshlands of Slapton Ley Nature Reserve, some pleasant woodland and a stretch along the Coast Path. On the final descent into Torcross a superb view unfolds along the length of Start Bay, with the whole of the route spread out before you. Historic interest ranges from the medieval church at Stokenham to a hitherto largely unknown Second World War disaster, commemorated by the tank at the start of the walk. The first 2½ miles (4km) are fairly flat; after that be prepared for several lengthy and fairly steep climbs.

The black Sherman tank at the south end of the car park was recovered from the seabed in 1984 and placed here as a memorial to over 900 US servicemen, killed by a surprise German attack in April 1944 while rehearsing for the D-Day landings. News of the tragedy was suppressed at the time and for many years it remained largely unknown until a local man, Ken Small, wrote a book about it and played a major role in organising the tank memorial.

At the north end of the car park a path leads off through a gate and runs parallel to, and just below, the road across the narrow causeway between the sea and the freshwater lagoon of Slapton Ley. After 1¼ miles (2km) the path reaches a lane. Turn left along this and after crossing Slapton Bridge turn left Ⓐ through a gate, at a public footpath sign, to follow a path through Slapton Ley Nature Reserve, an important habitat for wildfowl. The path, attractively tree-lined in places, keeps by the water and proceeds up and down steps, over stiles and across boardwalks. After bearing right along the right edge of a marshy area, you reach a fingerpost in front of a gate. Turn left Ⓑ, in the 'Permissive Route, Slapton Village' direction. Continue across more boardwalks, bending left along the left edge of the marsh to another fingerpost. Keep ahead, in 'Deer Bridge' direction, along a tree-lined path to emerge on to a lane Ⓒ.

Turn left over Deer Bridge and follow the lane steadily uphill for 1 mile (1.6km), curving gradually left to reach a junction of lanes at Coleridge Cross. At a public footpath sign Ⓓ bear to the left, then head diagonally right across a field, aiming for a tall footpath post. Go through a gate and continue straight across the next field to go through a gate on to a lane  **E** . Turn right downhill into Stokenham, an attractive village of whitewashed cottages, some of which are thatched, and presided over by an unusually large and imposing 15th-century church – a fine example of the Perpendicular style.

Like other villages in the area, Stokenham was evacuated in 1943 so that American troops could use it while making preparations for D-Day.

At a T-junction, turn right and almost immediately turn sharp left down a narrow, enclosed lane to another T-junction. Turn left (**Tradesmans Arms**

SCALE 1:27777 or 2¼ INCHES to 1 MILE 3.6CM to 1KM

| 0 | 200 | 400 | 600 | 800 METRES | 1 |
| KILOMETRES |
| MILES |
| 0 | 200 | 400 | 600 YARDS | ½ |

Stokenham

right) and follow the lane as it bends right to pass the church (**Church House Inn** right) to meet the main road **F**. Cross over, take the narrow, uphill lane opposite to a T-junction. Keep ahead through a metal kissing-gate, at a public footpath sign to Beeson, and continue uphill across a field towards a lone sycamore. Near the top keep by a wire fence on the right to go through another metal kissing-gate and continue to a tarmac track. Turn left along this through woodland. Opposite gates the track bears left and continues (signed 'Public Footpath') down to a thatched cottage. Follow a path to the left of the cottage and continue gently downhill along the left inside edge of woodland to a stile. Climb this, cross a track, climb another stile opposite and bear to the left to keep alongside the right edge of a sloping field.

Towards the field corner climb a stile on the right and continue down an enclosed path to reach a T-junction **G**.

Turn left to join the Coast Path, heading uphill through woodland, and follow this as it curves right, around the rim of Beesands Quarry, before descending to a gate. Go through the gate to emerge from the trees and continue downhill along a grassy path to another gate. From this path the view right to Beesands and Start Point, and later ahead over Start Bay, Slapton Sands and Slapton Ley is magnificent, and almost the whole route of the walk can be seen.

Go through the next gate and continue downhill along an enclosed path which eventually bends sharp right down to a tarmac track. Follow the track round a left bend and, at a waymarked post, turn sharp right. Walk along a gravel track, passing in front of houses, until this narrows to a path and descends steps to the promenade at Torcross. Continue along here, passing the **Seabreeze café** and **Start Bay Inn**, eventually turning left to reach the car park.

Fishing boats on the beach at Sidmouth

The Jurassic Coast

Dorset, one of the most unspoilt counties in the country – it has no motorways, and no large towns other than the Bournemouth–Poole conurbation – has another real claim to fame relating to its long and varied coast, along which runs the last leg of the South West Coast Path. In late 2001 a 95-mile (155km) stretch

Salcombe Hill Cliff and Sidmouth beach

from Old Harry Rocks near Purbeck west to Exmouth in Devon was designated England's first natural World Heritage Site, in the company of such world-famous sites as the Great Wall of China and Arizona's Grand Canyon. Popularly known as 'the Jurassic Coast', a walk from west to east along the Coast Path leads through bands of rock dating from the Triassic, Cretaceous and Jurassic Periods: the oldest rocks, at Orcombe Point near Exmouth, date back 250 million years.

There is a wealth of varied walking opportunities along its length. Much of

East Devon was dry and arid 200–250 million years ago, giving rise to the rusty red colour of its friable red sandstone cliffs. Moving east the white chalk cliffs of the Jurassic Coast are encountered, famed for their wealth of fossils, most famously around Lyme Regis and Charmouth in West Dorset. After stormy weather all manner of fossils can be found on the beaches there. And in the far east the chalk cliffs of the Isle of Purbeck give way to the sandy flats and heathlands bordering Poole Harbour.

But the walks given here – most within either the East Devon or Dorset AONBs – do more than celebrate the geological highlights of the Jurassic Coast. The delightful seaside resort of Sidmouth, which escaped Victorian 'modernisation' and retains a wealth of Georgian buildings, marks the starting point for an exploration of the surrounding steep combes and headlands. Golden Cap, at 626 feet (191m) the highest point on England's south coast, is scaled; the quiet and remote Isle of Purbeck, with its lofty ridges and Heritage Coast, explored. And the lovely village of Abbotsbury, home to the remains of a Benedictine monastery, an Iron Age hillfort, a swannery and nature reserve, includes a look at the extraordinary pebble bank of Chesil Beach, which runs for over 17 miles (28km) west along the coast from Portland.

Sidmouth & the Dunscombe Cliffs

The first part of the walk, a gentle stroll through a park beside the little River Sid, is the easiest. This is followed by a long, steady climb over Salcombe Hill to the attractive village of Salcombe Regis. Field paths lead on to the Donkey Sanctuary near the head of Weston Combe and then there is a gentle descent through the beautiful, well-wooded combe to the coast at Weston Mouth. The walk along the Coast Path back to Sidmouth is a strenuous, switchback route of nearly 3 miles (4.8km) over a series of steep and daunting-looking cliffs. Take your time and have frequent rests in order to enjoy the magnificent coastal views on this section of the walk, especially the view over Sidmouth on the final descent of Salcombe Hill Cliff.

Start
Sidmouth

Distance
8 miles (12.8km)

Height gain
1,345 feet (410m)

Approximate time
4 hours

Route terrain
Tracks, fields, some steep ascents: strenuous Coast Path with deep combes and steep ascents/descents

Parking
Car parks in Sidmouth (fee-paying)

Dog friendly
To be kept on leads through fields and Donkey Sanctuary; some non-dog-friendly stiles

OS maps
Landranger 192 (Exeter & Sidmouth), Explorer 115 (Exmouth & Sidmouth)

GPS waypoints
- SY 125 871
- **Ⓐ** SY 128 878
- **Ⓑ** SY 129 884
- **Ⓒ** SY 132 886
- **Ⓓ** SY 143 885
- **Ⓔ** SY 151 888
- **Ⓕ** SY 161 892
- **Ⓖ** SY 163 880

The genteel resort of Sidmouth occupies a sheltered position between steep red sandstone cliffs. It became fashionable during, and just after, the Napoleonic Wars when the English aristocracy were cut off from their usual continental haunts, and the town possesses a number of dignified Georgian and Regency villas, many of them now hotels. Royal prestige was bestowed on the town when the future Queen Victoria stayed here as a young girl with her parents in 1819.

The walk starts on the promenade, built in 1837, at the end of Station Road in front of the **Bedford Hotel**. Facing the beach turn left along the promenade, turn left just past **Hotel Elizabeth** and walk through the pedestrianised town centre; on meeting the High Street keep ahead. Opposite the Radway Cinema turn right along Salcombe Road; just after crossing the bridge over the River Sid turn left after the old Toll House **Ⓐ** along a tarmac path that continues through an attractive park beside the river for ½ mile (800m).

At a T-junction, turn right **Ⓑ** along a lane up to a road, turn left and where the road bears slightly right, bear right **Ⓒ** up hedged Milltown Lane. Where the lane ends continue uphill, at a 'public bridleway' sign, along an enclosed, tree-lined path. At a fork take the left-hand path and climb a flight of steps to a T-junction of paths and tracks. Turn left along a track heading steadily uphill through attractive woodland. The track bears right to emerge from the trees; keep ahead to eventually go through a gate and onto a road **Ⓓ**. Turn left, and at a fork by a war memorial, take the right-hand road and continue steeply

Looking towards Sidmouth from the Coast Path

downhill into Salcombe Regis, a quiet and secluded village of thatched cottages which has an attractive medieval church.

Just past the church turn right along a lane which heads uphill between trees. About 100 yards after emerging from the trees climb a stile on the left **E** at a pubic footpath sign. Walk along the left edge of a field, follow the field edge round to the right, climb a stile and keep ahead across a field to climb another. Continue along the left edge of the next field, climb the stile slightly to the left in the field corner (not the one in the hedge in front) and turn right through a kissing-gate. Keep ahead to pass through another, then two more close together. Continue along an avenue of memorial trees to pass through a kissing-gate on to a lane. Turn left and almost immediately right through a gate, following the pedestrian

route through the Donkey Sanctuary. This is a home for unwanted and neglected donkeys who are looked after for the rest of their lives and it is open to the public (free entry).

At a public footpath sign to Weston Mouth **F** keep ahead and walk downhill on a narrow path between wooden fences, climbing two stiles at the bottom. Turn right, signed to Weston Mouth, along a path that continues gently downhill through the beautiful, wooded Weston Combe, negotiating a gate and a stile en route. On meeting a track, bear left and continue downhill, eventually reaching a kissing-gate and a 'Coast Path' sign in the bottom left-hand corner of a

SCALE 1:25 000 or 2½ INCHES to 1 MILE 4CM to 1KM

0	200	400	600	800 METRES	1
					KILOMETRES
					MILES
0	200	400	600 YARDS	½

The start of the descent into Sidmouth

meadow. Turn right Ⓖ in the Salcombe Mouth direction, onto the Coast Path.

This is the start of the climb up Lower Dunscombe Cliff. Walk steeply uphill along the left edge of the meadow, following acorn symbols and passing a sign to Weston Plats. Go through the next gate and continue steeply up through trees and along a winding path. Turn sharp left, following the regular Coast Path acorn symbols, to emerge on to the open, grassy clifftop. The view to the east of Weston Cliff is particularly impressive. The path curves inland to a fingerpost, bears left down steps, heads up and bears left again to pass around the deep ravine of Lincombe, later rejoining the top of the cliffs and continuing along to Higher Dunscombe Cliff. Now come superb views looking westwards along the coast to Sidmouth with Torbay on the horizon.

A gate leads to the steep zigzag descent to Salcombe Mouth, stepped in places. Opposite is the daunting sight of Salcombe Hill Cliff. On entering the meadow the official route keeps ahead then turns right above the wooded combe to a fingerpost. Turn left, in the Sidmouth direction, to cross a footbridge over a stream and pass

through a kissing-gate. Turn left to keep above Salcombe Mouth.

Now follows one of the most energetic parts of the walk, the steep climb up Salcombe Hill Cliff. Continue along the clifftop, go through a gate and keep ahead to a viewfinder with a glorious view of Sidmouth before you. Follow the path as it curves right to a path junction by a seat; turn left on the Coast Path and descend steeply via steps through woodland, following acorn symbols ahead all the time. Finally the path crosses a big meadow, descending all the while. At this point the Coast Path has been diverted because of unstable cliffs ahead. Turn right to join an enclosed tarmac path that runs into a narrow lane.

At the end of this turn left down Laskeys Lane between houses. Where the lane bends right, bear left along another tarmac track, and where this ends turn right downhill along a road (Cliff Road). Where the road bends right, keep ahead along a tarmac path which curves left to rejoin the original line of the Coast Path. Bear right and follow the path to cross a bridge over the River Sid. Keep ahead on the promenade to return to the start. ●

Golden Cap

Start
Seatown

Distance
6½ miles (10.5km)

Height gain
1,675 feet (510m)

Approximate time
4 hours

Route terrain
Undulating fields and tracks; stiff final climb onto Golden Cap

Parking
Car park at Seatown (fee-paying), 3½ miles (5.5km) south-west of Bridport

Dog friendly
To be kept on leads through fields; some non-dog-friendly stiles

OS maps
Landranger 193 (Taunton & Lyme Regis), Explorer 116 (Lyme Regis & Bridport)

GPS waypoints
SY 420 918
Ⓐ SY 414 921
Ⓑ SY 401 924
Ⓒ SY 389 935
Ⓓ SY 381 932
Ⓔ SY 385 927
Ⓕ SY 407 922

Most of the coast between the villages of Seatown and Charmouth is owned by the National Trust, and a combination of clear, well-maintained paths and good waymarking, plus the outstanding cliff scenery and spectacular views along the coast and inland, make this excellent walking country. Golden Cap is, at 626 feet (191m), the highest point on the south coast of England and is inevitably a superb viewpoint. Its name comes from the layer of golden sandstone that crowns its distinctive flat summit. This is quite an energetic walk, with several ascents and descents, but the only stiff climb is the final one, up to the top of Golden Cap itself, which is the highlight of the walk.

Crumbling cliffs have taken with them some sections of Dorset's coastal path, the clifftop path route shown on older maps climbing west from the beach at Seatown being one of them. Therefore, follow the lane inland from the car park, leaving some 100 yards beyond the bend over a stile on the left. A contained path, signed as the Coast Path Diversion leads to a kissing-gate and on across a crop field. Over a plank bridge, dodge through a clump of trees, cross a stile and pass through another kissing-gate. Head up to join the original route at a fingerpost by a seat. Signed right to Golden Cap the way continues upwards to another junction Ⓐ.

Directed by a sign to Langdon Hill and Chideock, bear right off the Coast Path and walk on to a stile some 50 yards ahead. Keep climbing by the right-hand fence to a stile in front of the dark woodlands of Langdon Hill.

Follow the path left at the edge of the wood. Pass through a gate at the end of the trees and keep beside the left hedge. Reaching the corner, ignore the stile and instead swing right looking for a gate some 50 yards farther on. Turn through that and again stay by the left hedge. Inland, the view is to the rolling downs, while ahead Lyme Regis can be seen across the bay.

A fingerpost in the corner points right towards St Gabriel's Wood. Approaching the trees, leave through a gate on the left and walk away at the bottom of the field on a developing track that leads past the restored remains of St Gabriel's Church. The small 13th-century church served the Saxon settlement of

Stanton St Gabriel.

Over a stile, carry on to a junction by a fine thatched farmhouse **B** and take the track right towards Morcombelake and Stonebarrow. Over a stream, it climbs between the fields, later swinging right and eventually reaching a junction of tracks at the end of Muddyford Lane. To the left, the way is signed to Stonebarrow and Charmouth and rises to Upcot Farm.

In the yard, go right past the farmhouse and, ignoring a later path off right, continue to a fork. Keeping with the right branch, walk on along the track, passing through a couple of gates and curving left. Eventually climbing a stile, bear right gaining height across open grass and gorse to a small parking area **C**.

To the left a broad track falls along the crest of Stonebarrow Hill. There are fine views to the coast and then across Marshwood Vale to the hills of west Dorset before the track reaches another parking area, where there is a seasonal

National Trust shop and information point.

At the far end of the car park **D**, turn off left and head downhill on a broad grass path at the edge of gorse heath. Lower down, ignore a crossing path, but later curve left, soon meeting a concrete track. Signed right towards the Coast Path, it leads down to Westhay Farm. Keep ahead past the buildings on a grass path, passing

Approaching Golden Cap, the highest point on the south coast of England

through a gate and striking across open pasture to a fingerpost 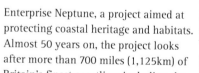 E.

Now joining the Coast Path, follow it left towards Seatown. The route drops to cross Westhay Water and continues over a rise to cross Ridge Water. A stepped path climbs away and runs over Broom Cliff. After crossing a final stream above Gabriel's Mouth, the way settles into the final long pull on to the top of Golden Cap.

The distinctive 'Golden Cap' is a layer of sandstone crowning the mudstone bulk of the crumbling hill, which weathers to a lovely warm honey colour. Landslip and wave erosion incessantly eat at the cliffs, washing out countless fossils on to the beach below. On the summit is a memorial to the Earl of Antrim, who was Chairman of the National Trust from 1966 until his death in 1977. One of his great concerns was the ongoing loss of coastline to development and he helped launch

Enterprise Neptune, a project aimed at protecting coastal heritage and habitats. Almost 50 years on, the project looks after more than 700 miles (1,125km) of Britain's finest coastline, including the section here. The climb to the top might have been strenuous, but the view is tremendous and extends from Portland Bill to the distant Devon coast.

Just beyond the triangulation pillar F a stepped path drops steeply from the top. Over a stile, the Coast Path to Seatown is signed to the right. Following waymarks carry on down the hill, ultimately picking up your outward track back to the village. ●

SCALE 1:25000 or 2½ INCHES to 1 MILE 4CM to 1KM

Abbotsbury & Chesil Beach

Start
Abbotsbury

Distance
6¼ miles (10.1km)

Height gain
1,115 feet (340m)

Approximate time
3½ hours

Route terrain
Ridge-top path, undulating fields and tracks, level Coast Path by Chesil Beach

Parking
Car park at Abbotsbury (fee-paying), signed off B3157

Dog friendly
To be kept on leads through fields; some non-dog-friendly stiles

OS maps
Landranger 194 (Dorchester & Weymouth), Explorer OL15 (Purbeck & South Dorset)

GPS waypoints
  SY 578 852
Ⓐ SY 578 854
Ⓑ SY 572 862
Ⓒ SY 550 865
Ⓓ SY 546 854
Ⓔ SY 567 846
Ⓕ SY 575 851

Part of the World Heritage Jurassic Coast, the stark, straight run of Chesil Beach is a marked contrast to the miles of meandering cliffs on either side. It is incorporated in this enjoyable ramble from Abbotsbury, which first climbs on to the open and windswept downs to the prehistoric Abbotsbury Castle. After an impressive stretch beside Chesil Beach, the way turns inland around Chapel Hill back to the village. The energetic but optional ascent to the tiny hilltop chapel makes a fitting finale to the walk.

The abbey that gave the village its name was founded under Benedictine rule in 1044 by Orc, a steward of King Cnut. Its dedication to St Peter echoes a tradition dating to the first chapel constructed in the 5th century by Bertulfus, a priest to whom the saint appeared in visions. The abbey's fortunes fluctuated, but its medieval prosperity is reflected in a massive tithe barn that was erected to the south of the church, one of the few buildings to remain after the monastery was dissolved in 1539. Another monastic survivor is the Swannery at the head of the Fleet Lagoon. The long, narrow lake contained behind the shingle bank of Chesil Beach is a natural breeding ground for birds and, in addition to the more traditional practices of fishing and farming, the monks began managing its flock of mute swans as a source of meat. The thriving colony has over 150 breeding pairs and is a popular visitor attraction, particularly during May and June when the cygnets hatch from their eggs.

🖌 Leave the car park at its northern entrance, crossing to Rosemary Lane opposite. At the top, go left along Back Street, turning off right after 100 yards between thatched cottages along Blind Lane, a track signed to the Hill Fort and Hardy Monument Ⓐ. Curving left and then swinging sharply right, it climbs more steeply between hedge-banks. Through a gate, carry on across open grassland to reach another gate, from which there is a superb view back to Abbotsbury village, the church, tithe barn and St Catherine's Chapel on its hilltop. Beyond the gate, keep ahead across a field, making for another gate and fingerpost in a hedge. Now bear slightly left, following signs to Hill Fort, and continue along a rising grassy path between outcrops of rock. Maintain a straight line, heading towards another fingerpost at the top of the ridge **B**.

Here turn left to join the inland section of the Dorset Coast Path, soon passing through a gate. Carry on along this superb path that runs across the top of the broad, grassy ridge, which offers stunning views to the left over the coast and to the right across rolling downland. Passing by several tumuli, ignore a track that bears left to the road below and walk on, finally reaching a gate out to a lane. From the small parking area opposite, a footpath signed to West Bexington, climbs between gorse bushes and over a stile towards the earthworks of Abbotsbury Castle.

Triangular in plan and protected by double ramparts and a deep ditch, the fort occupies a commanding spot. It could provide early warning of any invasion from the sea and was no doubt an outpost of Maiden Castle farther inland.

However, there is no evidence that it offered any great resistance to the Roman legions when they landed in AD43.

The path follows the line of the southern ramparts and eventually descends along a narrowing ridge. Continue parallel to the road over a grassy knoll before leaving through a gate in the far corner of a field on to the carriageway **C**.

Cross to a gate and stile on to the National Trust's Tulk's Hill. Follow the wall to a fingerpost at its corner and go left towards Chesil Beach. A grass path leads downhill at the edge of a gorse heath to reach another fingerpost. Keep left, winding through scrub to enter the corner of a field over a stile. Stride downhill beside the hedge to the bottom corner by Labour-in-Vain Farm.

Over a stile and guided by a yellow

SCALE 1:29412 or 2¼ INCHES to 1 MILE 3.4CM to 1KM

waymark, bear half-right across a field to a gate in the far corner by East Bexington Farm. Passing through a second gate, the ongoing track curves right to skirt the farm buildings. Ignoring a crossing track, keep ahead to a gate and continue down the edge of a field towards the sea.

On reaching the coast **D**, turn left along a rough tarmac track running behind the high embankment of Chesil Beach and signposted as the Coast Path to Abbotsbury.

The high bank of shingle and pebbles runs for 18 miles (29km) in an almost straight line from West Bay near Bridport to the Isle of Portland. At its eastern end, it encloses a long, narrow saltwater lake, the Fleet Lagoon, which attracts huge numbers of wading birds throughout the year, particularly at breeding time. There is an ongoing debate over the origin of the spit, one of the longest in the world, and it has been suggested that it is actually two separate beaches. Curious is the fact that the pebbles from which the bank is formed are perfectly graded along its length, from tiny gravel at West Bay to fist-size cobbles at Portland. It was said that local fishermen landing at night could tell exactly where they were along the beach from the size of the pebbles.

At the point where the tarmac lane subsequently turns inland past a car park, keep ahead through a gate along a shingle path. Stay with the hedge and path as they curve from the sea around the perimeter of the Fleet Sanctuary Nature Reserve, bringing St Catherine's Chapel into view on the hilltop ahead. Ignore a green-arrowed permissive path on the right, but at the next fingerpost **E**, turn right over a stile, following a sign 'Coast Path and Swannery'. Joining the right-hand fence, walk up to a gate and carry on along the grassy path ahead,

The swans of Abbotsbury Swannery

from which there is a fine view beyond the Swannery across the lagoon to Chesil Beach. As the Swannery car park appears ahead, bear left to climb a stile into woodland. The path contours the hill, leaving the trees over another stile.

Continue along the path towards Abbotsbury, but just before reaching a metal kissing-gate **F**, turn sharp left on a climbing track to St Catherine's Chapel at the top of the hill. The ½ mile (800m) diversion is satisfyingly worthwhile, both for the chapel itself and for the views from its hilltop site.

The chapel was built around 1400 by the monks of Abbotsbury Abbey and was probably used by visitors as a place of prayer before descending to the abbey itself. After the Dissolution, the chapel was retained, probably because of its value as a landmark for sailors. It has an almost fortress-like appearance with great buttresses, and it is noted for its rare, stone, tunnel-vaulted roof. The all-round panorama is splendid, especially that looking towards Abbotsbury, cradled below amidst the downs and dominated by its church.

From the chapel, retrace your steps to rejoin the main route at the bottom of the hill **F**. Passing through the metal kissing-gate, walk on along a broad track to the road. Turn right towards the village and bear left at the first junction to return along Back Street to the car park. ●

Lulworth Cove & Durdle Door

walk 25

Start
Lulworth Cove

Distance
5 miles (8km)

Height gain
1,575 feet (480m)

Approximate time
3 hours.

Route terrain
Rolling downland, fields, undulating and popular Coast Path past Durdle Door

Parking
Car park at Lulworth Cove (fee-paying), signed off B3070

Dog friendly
To be kept on leads through fields; some non-dog-friendly stiles

OS maps
Landranger 194 (Dorchester & Weymouth), Explorer OL15 (Purbeck & South Dorset)

GPS waypoints
SY 824 799
Ⓐ SY 828 801
Ⓑ SY 829 797
Ⓒ SY 829 802
Ⓓ SY 821 803
Ⓔ SY 811 810
Ⓕ SY 802 804

The last mile (1.6km) of this walk is along the most popular stretch of the Dorset coast, best avoided at bank holidays and other peak times. The reasons for its popularity are obvious: the attractive Lulworth Cove, the geological phenomenon of Durdle Door, and the magnificent cliff scenery in between. The walk also explores some fine countryside inland and provides an optional detour to the fascinating Fossil Forest, which is just inside the boundary of the Lulworth Army Ranges. Although only a short walk, it has several steep climbs.

Note: For information on access and the absolute need to observe the warning notices, see Walk 26.

From the car park, head back left up the road for 200 yards. If the range is open, to reach the fossil forest, take a path climbing away on the right beside the last house. Breaking out on to the down, turn right with the Coast Path. Continue above the cliffs backing Lulworth Cove until the path levels to a T-junction Ⓐ.

The Lulworth coast is one of the most geologically interesting in the country, where striation, folding and spectacular marine erosion can all be seen in just a short walk. Rock bands of differing hardness have been tilted to near vertical, with Lulworth Cove forming behind a narrow breach in the resistant limestone fronting the coast. The incoming sea has eroded the softer rock behind, the breaking waves curving to create the

Lulworth Cove

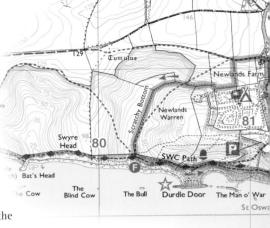

almost circular bay seen today. A similar process is taking place at neighbouring Stair Hole, but is at a much earlier stage. However, farther along the coast either side of Durdle Door, erosion is almost complete and, except for a narrow stub protecting an isthmus of the softer beds, the outer bands have all but been washed away with the coastline now along the more resistant chalk behind. The 'Door' will eventually succumb to the waves, but for the time being remains an impressive feature.

Go through a gate on the right and follow a stepped path down to a Coast Path marker stone. Following signs for Pelper Point and Fossil Forest, go left and right passing the meagre remains of the 13th-century Little Bindon Chapel, hidden in the undergrowth to the left. The Coast Path eventually turns from Lulworth Cove to the range boundary. Pass through and then look for another marker **B**, where the Fossil Forest is signed down steps to the beach.

Some 145 million years ago, towards the end of the Jurassic period, rising sea levels flooded an ancient forest. The stumps of trees and fallen trunks were encased in algae and mud, which subsequently became preserved as fossils.

Retrace your steps along the Coast Path, climbing back to the

Durdle Door

gate at point **A**. Now keep ahead beside the fence to a junction at the top of the hill by another gate on to the Army Range **C**. There, go left along a broad grass swathe signed towards Lulworth. Steadily descending, intersect a path and go right, but then in 100 yards watch for another descending path off left. Continue downhill, aiming left of farm buildings on the other side of the valley. Over a stile, follow the path back down to the road.

Turn right, but abandon the lane after some 50 yards through a gap in the left hedge **D**. Walk away at the field edge, crossing a stile, to reach another. Climb that, go up steps to a gate, and bear right along a footpath signed to Durdle Door. Beyond another gate, follow a grassy track along the lower slopes of Hambury Tout. Carry on steadily uphill to reach the edge of a caravan site. Opening the gate, turn right through the site, passing the reception to leave along the main drive.

Reaching a sharp bend **E**, turn left into Newlands Farm. Go right between the buildings and then left along a track. After 150 yards at a sign to Scratchy Bottom, enter the field on the left and head down beside the boundary. Swing right within the bottom corner above the caravan site and follow waymarks in the next corner to a gate. A track leads away, with the fence first on the left and then on the right, curving downhill to follow the oddly-named valley towards the coast.

Through a gate at the end **F**, join the Coast Path and go left. Breasting the rise brings the arresting sight of Durdle Door into view. The way continues across the down behind the next bay before turning up towards the caravan site. Higher up, watch for the Coast Path leaving through a gate on the right. A broad path rises across the flank of Hambury Tout. As the way then begins to lose height, Lulworth Cove dominates the final stages of the walk back to the car park. ●

walk 26

Start
Tyneham

Distance
3½ miles (5.6km)

Height gain
935 feet (285m)

Approximate time
2 hours

Route terrain
Downland ridges and fields, undulating Coast Path, steep ascent onto Gad Cliff

Parking
Picnic area at Tyneham (honesty box), 6 miles (9.5km) west of Corfe Castle

Dog friendly
Under control at all times; some non-dog-friendly stiles

OS maps
Landranger 194 (Dorchester & Weymouth), Explorer OL15 (Purbeck & South Dorset)

GPS waypoints
SY 881 802
Ⓐ SY 881 810
Ⓑ SY 865 805
Ⓒ SY 884 796

Tyneham & Worbarrow Bay

The hidden fold of the Tyneham valley cleaves the western end of the Purbeck Hills to a superb beach behind Worbarrow Bay. Used for army training since 1943 it has not been subject to intensive farming and is consequently rich in plant and wildlife. This short but energetic circuit climbs from the abandoned village on to the ridge before returning along the dramatic Jurassic Coast.

Range access is restricted, but coastal footpaths and Tyneham village are open most weekends, bank holidays and during the summer holiday. Check www.dorsetforyou.com or call 01929 404819 for up-to-date information.

Note: Waymarking is excellent and the route is easy to follow, but as the frequent warning notices tell you, it is essential to use only the permitted paths and tracks and always to keep within the line of regular yellow-topped posts because of the danger of unexploded shells.

Tyneham is a ghost village, deserted since 1943 when the War Office took over the surrounding area, initially as a training ground for Allied troops preparing for the D-Day Normandy landings. The Victorian church, schoolroom and other abandoned, partially ruined buildings give it a movingly melancholy air. It is also a place of great historic curiosity, and an exhibition in the church tells the history of this unusual museum piece.

From the car park, walk back towards the village, bearing left and then right to climb away on a path behind the church. It heads straight up the hill, in time bending right as the gradient steepens. At a junction just before reaching the road Ⓐ, go left to follow a track over the crest of Whiteway Hill. In springtime the slopes are washed with the blue and yellow of bluebells and gorse, while fine views extend to the coast and across the heath to East Lulworth's church and castle.

Where the track later swings right, keep ahead along the crest of the ridge, shortly reaching the boundary of Flower's Barrow Iron Age fort. Pass through a gap in the embankment, but then at a footpath sign Ⓑ, go left. Re-cross the earthwork to a stile and head steeply downhill. There is a superb scene to the west of the switchback cliffs stretching into the distance beyond

Lulworth Cove, while ahead is a magnificent picture over Worbarrow Bay. Climb a stile to descend to the beach, passing the ruins of fishermen's cottages.

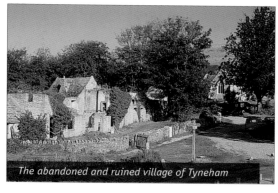

The abandoned and ruined village of Tyneham

Cross a footbridge spanning a stream and go left on a rising track. After a few yards turn right up steps and continue across a level area of grass to a kissing-gate. The way carries on steeply uphill along the edge of Gad Cliff, which although a strenuous pull, rewards your effort with fine views over the Tyneham valley and along the Dorset coast.

Shortly after crossing a stile, look out for a stone footpath marker **C**. Turn left and walk to a stile, continuing downhill with the ongoing path. Reaching the bottom, bear left across a field to a stile by a cattle-grid at the far side. Follow the track ahead between trees to return to the car park. ●

SCALE 1:25 000 or 2½ INCHES to 1 MILE 4CM to 1KM

Kimmeridge Bay & Swyre Head

Start
Kimmeridge

Distance
8¾ miles (14.1km)

Height gain
1,395 feet (425m)

Approximate time
5 hours

Route terrain
Undulating Coast Path, steep climb onto Swyre Head; inland tracks, fields and ridge-top paths

Parking
Quarry car park just above and north-east of village

Dog friendly
To be kept on leads through fields; some non-dog-friendly stiles

OS maps
Landranger 195 (Bournemouth & Purbeck), Explorer OL15 (Purbeck & South Dorset)

GPS waypoints
SY 919 800
Ⓐ SY 915 796
Ⓑ SY 908 792
Ⓒ SY 950 773
Ⓓ SY 953 795
Ⓔ SY 943 792
Ⓕ SY 933 785

After a short walk across fields from Kimmeridge to the coast, there follows a lovely cliff-top trek above Kimmeridge Ledges, a remarkable stretch of wave-cut platform and part of the Jurassic Coast World Heritage Site. After a short but stiff pull on to Houns-tout Cliff, the route turns inland to Kingston and climbs steadily on to the superb viewpoint of Swyre Head. A glorious gentle descent along the down to Smedmore Hill provides a fitting conclusion to this grand ramble.

From the car park above Kimmeridge, turn right along the lane to a junction, where a footpath signed to Kimmeridge leaves over a stile on the left. A pleasant, grassy path, from which there are fine views to the coast, heads downhill into the village. Go through a metal kissing-gate into the churchyard and pass left of the small church.

The church has an early Norman foundation, and although now dedicated to St Nicholas, the name of its original patron saint has been lost. It was never blessed with a tower and the bell hangs from a small bellcote above the western gable. The church, substantially rebuilt in 1872, contains memorials to the Clavells of nearby Smedmore House and a 12th-century font, discovered lying in a hedge in 1920.

Emerging on to the bend of a lane, walk ahead through the village, passing The Etches Collection of locally found fossils. Beside the last thatched cottage on the right, climb a stile **A** and stride away at the field edge towards Kimmeridge Bay and the Coast Path. Over a footbridge, turn left and keep with the meandering boundary beside a succession of fields, ultimately coming out on to a narrow lane **B**. Turn left towards a parking field, crossing that to the Coast Path running along the top of the low cliffs above Kimmeridge Bay. Follow it left around the curve of the bay, eventually meeting a tarmac track. Go right, down towards the Marine Centre, but then turn off left, up a flight of steps on to Hen Cliff. At the top, carry on past the prominent landmark of Clavell Tower.

Held by the Clavells since the early 15th century, the Smedmore estate eventually passed to the Reverend John Richards Clavell in 1818 who built the

tower. For a century it served as a summerhouse and lookout but, abandoned after the Great War, fell into dereliction and by the end of the 20th century, was in danger of crumbling with the cliff into the sea. Following a much-publicised appeal, work began in 2006 to dismantle and relocate the tower farther from the edge. Now in the care of the Landmark Trust and restored to its former glory, it is a striking landmark on this beautiful coastline.

The route follows the undulating clifftop for the next 3 miles (4.8km), a particularly attractive stretch of coast that looks spectacularly towards St Aldhelm's Head. Approaching Egmont

SCALE 1:29412 or 2¼ INCHES to 1 MILE 3.4CM to 1KM

0	200	400	600	800 METRES	**1**
					KILOMETRES
					MILES
0	200	400	600 YARDS	**½**	

A grassy path descends into Kimmeridge

Bight, where a waterfall drops into the sea, the path descends before climbing steeply on to Houns-tout Cliff. Pause at the strategically sited stone seat for a retrospective view to the Isle of Portland, before turning inland by a marker stone **C** towards Kingston.

Over a stile, walk away above the Encombe valley, which cradles Encombe Dairy and Encombe House within its deep fold. Keep going over more stiles, picking up a track at the edge of Quarry Wood and entering The Plantation. Stay with the main track, bearing right at the edge of Encombe estate and following signs to Kingston to emerge on to a lane **D**. The village and the **Scott Arms** are a short detour to the right.

The village has two 19th-century churches. The original church, a chapelry of Corfe Castle, stood at the eastern end of the village and was erected in the 12th century. It was rebuilt by the first Earl of Eldon in 1833, but in 1921 became redundant when a 'new' church, begun in 1874 as a private chapel for the third Earl, was adopted as the parish church. Sometimes described as a miniature cathedral, it is an elaborate and majestic building and was designed by George Edmund Street. Fascinated by the Gothic style, Street developed his skills under Sir George Scott and became a noted architect in his own right, later employing the young William Morris as an apprentice. Much of his work was carried out on churches, but he also designed the Royal Courts of Justice in London.

Return to **D** and follow the ongoing lane, which soon breaks from trees to give an impressive view to the Purbeck Hills and Corfe Castle. Reaching a small car park **E**, turn left between stone gateposts and then bear right through a waymarked gate. After crossing open pasture, continue at the edge of Polar Wood and then climb on to Swyre Head.

Swyre Head is the highest point of the Purbeck Hills and gives a far-reaching panorama that extends from Dartmoor to the Isle of Wight. The prominent mound is a prehistoric tumulus, its top flattened to provide the base for a windmill that has long-since gone.

Walk past the triangulation pillar **G** and through a gate beyond to follow the crest of the ridge over Smedmore Hill. The glorious views make a grand finale to the walk, the path finally descending to a lane. Go left and left again the short distance back to the car park. ●

Ballard Down & Old Harry

There is plenty of variety on this walk, which includes the largest remaining area of open heathland in Dorset, the breezy chalk headland of Ballard Down flanked by Studland and Swanage Bays, and a coastal stretch that passes by distinctive Old Harry Rocks. Two other features are the Agglestone Rock and the little church at Studland. Much of the walk is on National Trust land.

Start	Studland
Distance	6¼ miles (10.1km)
Height gain	1,100 feet (335m)
Approximate time	3½ hours
Route terrain	Heathland tracks, downland, undemanding Coast Path
Parking	Studland NT car park 3½ miles (5.5km) north of Swanage
Dog friendly	To be kept on leads through fields; some non-dog-friendly stiles
OS maps	Landranger 195 (Bournemouth & Purbeck), Explorer OL15 (Purbeck & South Dorset)
GPS waypoints	SZ 037 825
	Ⓐ SZ 032 824
	Ⓑ SZ 017 818
	Ⓒ SZ 020 816
	Ⓓ SZ 054 824

Leaving the car park entrance, turn left and immediately left again through a gate along a path to St Nicholas' Church.

Of Saxon origin, the present building is largely Norman and dates from the early 12th century, its curious squat tower capped with a saddle-back roof and appearing decidedly unfinished. Interesting too are the rows of carved corbels sheltering beneath the eaves of the nave roof, amongst which you will find a sheela na gig. These blatantly rude carvings appear on churches up and down the country and, while commonly assumed to be of pagan origin, their true significance remains a mystery.

Follow the path through the graveyard past the church, continuing beyond to emerge on to a lane. Go right to a crossroads and carry on along Heath Green Road opposite. After 200 yards, a bridleway leaves on the right beside a small playing field Ⓐ. Ignoring side paths, keep with it to a T-junction at its end and walk right, soon coming out on to a rough lane.

Turn left, passing between farmhouses and through a gate into woodland. Follow a bridleway sign to Agglestone Rock over a footbridge then bear left on to the edge of Godlingston Heath. Take the first path off left and head towards the Agglestone Rock, which appears on the ridge ahead.

Some 17 feet (5m) high, the huge rock weighs around 400 tons and is a remnant of ferruginous sandstone that once covered the area. More resistant than the underlying rock, it sheltered the base from erosion and until recently, the boulder balanced upon a pedestal like a great anvil. According to legend, the Devil hurled it at Corfe Castle from the Isle of Wight. The spot is a grand viewpoint, looking north across the heath to Poole Harbour and Bournemouth. The largest area of unspoiled heathland in the county, Godlingston and Studland are fragments of the great heath that once covered much of eastern Dorset and the inspiration for Hardy's *Egdon Heath*.

Beyond the rock, continue with the sandy track across the undulating heath to a junction by a National Trust waymark stone. To the right, walk through double gates in the direction of Studland Road. Following bridleway signs, branch right at a fork and remain with the main track, which shortly crosses a golf course. At a junction near the top of the hill bear right and then keep ahead to pass out through a gate on to Studland Road **B**.

Turn left, but almost immediately go right over a stile. Strike out across another part of the golf course, making for a yellow-topped post marking the onward path into the trees. Continue downhill to a stile and bear right across an overgrown field to another stile in the bottom right corner. Emerging on to a lane, follow the verge left around a bend before turning off right along a

track **C**.

Through a gate, it climbs across fields on to the down, later curving left to reach an obelisk from which there are views right and left to Swanage and Bournemouth. Ahead across the intervening sea is

Old Harry Rocks

the Isle of Wight.

From the obelisk, carry on with the obvious track, shortly passing through a gate to continue along the crest of Ballard Down. Ignore a later crossing path and keep going, eventually reaching a triangulation pillar. There bear right and then left to join the Coast Path, which falls gently down to Ballard Point. Swinging left it stays above the cliffs, passing The Pinnacles to the point above Old Harry 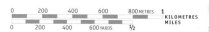.

In the 18th century, The Foreland and Old Harry were still connected to the mainland. Erosion over time has separated them, the sea piercing arches through the chalk, which have since collapsed to create distinct islands. The process inexorably continues; Old

Harry's wife collapsed in 1896 to leave the stump we see today and Old Harry, the outermost stack, will inevitably suffer the same fate. The Needles off the Isle of Wight are part of the same geological feature, the intervening rock having been worn away at the end of the last ice age.

Rounding the point, the path now curves west back above another run of cliffs towards Studland. Approaching the edge of the village, take the right fork, a contained track that descends to the road. Turn right, walking past the **Bankes Arms** to return to the car park.

SCALE 1:25000 or 2½ INCHES to 1 MILE 4CM to 1KM

Further Information

Walking Safety

Although the reasonably gentle countryside that is the subject of this book offers no real dangers to walkers at any time of the year, it is still advisable to take sensible precautions and follow certain well-tried guidelines.

Always take with you both warm and waterproof clothing and sufficient food and drink. Wear suitable footwear, such as strong walking boots or shoes that give a good grip over stony ground, on slippery slopes and in muddy conditions. Try to obtain a local weather forecast and bear it in mind before you start. Do not be afraid to abandon your proposed route and return to your starting point in the event of a sudden and unexpected deterioration in the weather.

All the walks described in this book will be safe to do, given due care and respect, even during the winter. Indeed, a crisp, fine winter day often provides perfect walking conditions, with firm ground underfoot and a clarity unique to this time of the year. The most difficult hazard likely to be encountered is mud, especially when walking along woodland and field paths, farm tracks and bridleways – the latter in particular can often get churned up by cyclists and horses. In summer, an additional difficulty may be narrow and overgrown paths, particularly along the edges of cultivated fields. Always ensure appropriate footwear is worn.

Walkers and the Law

The Countryside and Rights of Way Act (CRoW Act 2000) gives a public right of access in England and Wales to land mapped as open country (mountain, moor, heath and down) or registered common land. These areas are known as *open access land*, and include land around the coastline, known as *coastal margin*.

Where You Can Go
Rights of Way
Prior to the introduction of the CRoW Act, walkers could only legally access the countryside along public rights of way. These are either 'footpaths' (for walkers only) or 'bridleways' (for walkers, riders on horseback and pedal cyclists). A third category called 'Byways open to all traffic' (BOATs), is used by motorised vehicles as well as those using non-mechanised transport. Mainly they are green lanes, farm and estate roads, although occasionally they will be found crossing mountainous area.

Rights of way are marked on Ordnance Survey maps. Look for the green broken lines on the Explorer maps, or the red dashed lines on Landranger maps.

The term 'right of way' means exactly what it says. It gives a right of passage over what, for the most part, is private land. Under pre-CRoW legislation walkers were required to keep to the line of the right of way and not stray onto land on either side. If you did inadvertently wander off the right of way, either because of faulty map reading or because the route was not clearly indicated on the ground, you were technically trespassing.

Local authorities have a legal obligation to ensure that rights of way are kept clear and free of obstruction, and are signposted where they leave metalled roads. The duty of local authorities to install signposts extends to the placing of signs along a path or way, but only where the authority considers it necessary to have a signpost or waymark to assist persons unfamiliar with the locality.

CRoW Access Rights
Access Land
As well as being able to walk on existing rights of way, under CRoW legislation you have access to large areas of open land and under further legislation, a right of coastal access, which is being implemented by Natural England, giving for the first time the right of access around all England's

Countryside Access Charter

Your rights of way are:

- public footpaths – on foot only. Sometimes waymarked in yellow
- bridle-ways – on foot, horseback and pedal cycle. Sometimes waymarked in blue
- byways (usually old roads), most 'roads used as public paths' and, of course, public roads – all traffic has the right of way

Use maps, signs and waymarks to check rights of way. Ordnance Survey Explorer and Landranger maps show most public rights of way

On rights of way you can:

- take a pram, pushchair or wheelchair if practicable
- take a dog (on a lead or under close control)
- take a short route round an illegal obstruction or remove it sufficiently to get past

You have a right to go for recreation to:

- public parks and open spaces – on foot
- most commons near older towns and cities – on foot and sometimes on horseback
- private land where the owner has a formal agreement with the local authority

In addition you can use the following by local or established custom or consent, but ask for advice if you are unsure:

- many areas of open country, such as moorland, fell and coastal areas, especially those in the care of the National Trust, and some commons
- some woods and forests, especially those owned by Forestry England
- country parks and picnic sites
- most beaches
- canal towpaths
- some private paths and tracks Consent sometimes extends to horse-riding and cycling

For your information:

- county councils and London boroughs maintain and record rights of way, and register commons
- obstructions, dangerous animals, harassment and misleading signs on rights of way are illegal and you should report them to the county council
- paths across fields can be ploughed, but must normally be reinstated within two weeks
- landowners can require you to leave land to which you have no right of access
- motor vehicles are normally permitted only on roads, byways and some 'roads used as public paths'

---

open coast. This includes plans for an England Coast Path (ECP) which will run for 2,795 miles (4,500 kilometres). A corresponding Wales Coast Path has been open since 2012.

Coastal access rights apply within the coastal margin (including along the ECP) unless the land falls into a category of excepted land or is subject to local restrictions, exclusions or diversions.

You can of course continue to use rights of way to cross access land, but you can lawfully leave the path and wander at will in these designated areas.

Where to Walk

Access Land is shown on Ordnance Survey Explorer maps by a light yellow tint surrounded by a pale orange border. New orange coloured 'i' symbols on the maps will show the location of permanent access information boards installed by the access authorities. Coastal Margin is shown on Ordnance Survey Explorer maps by a pink tint.

Restrictions

The right to walk on access land may lawfully be restricted by landowners. Landowners can, for any reason, restrict access for up to 28 days in any year. They cannot however close the land:

- on bank holidays;
- for more than four Saturdays and Sundays in a year;
- on any Saturday from 1 June to 11 August; or
- on any Sunday from 1 June to the end

of September.

They have to provide local authorities with five working days' notice before the date of closure unless the land involved is an area of less than five hectares or the closure is for less than four hours. In these cases landowners only need to provide two hours' notice.

Whatever restrictions are put into place on access land they have no effect on existing rights of way, and you can continue to walk on them.

Dogs

Dogs can be taken on access land, but must be kept on leads of two metres or less between 1 March and 31 July, and at all times where they are near livestock. In addition landowners may impose a ban on all dogs from fields where lambing takes place for up to six weeks in any year. Dogs may be banned from moorland used for grouse shooting and breeding for up to five years.

General Obstructions

Obstructions can sometimes cause a problem on a walk and the most common of these is where the path across a field has been ploughed over. It is legal for a farmer to plough up a path provided that it is restored within two weeks. This does not always happen and you are faced with the dilemma of following the line of the path, even if this means treading on crops, or walking round the edge of the field. Although the latter course of action seems the most sensible, it does mean that you would be trespassing.

Other obstructions can vary from overhanging vegetation to wire fences across the path, locked gates or even a cattle feeder on the path.

Use common sense. If you can get round the obstruction without causing damage, do so. Otherwise only remove as much of the obstruction as is necessary to secure passage.

If the right of way is blocked and cannot be followed, there is a long-standing view that in such circumstances there is a right to deviate, but this cannot wholly be relied on. Although it is accepted in law that highways (and that includes rights of way) are for the

public service, and if the usual track is impassable, it is for the general good that people should be entitled to pass into another line. However, this should not be taken as indicating a right to deviate whenever a way is impassable. If in doubt, retreat.

Report obstructions to the local authority and/or the Ramblers.

 ## Useful Organisations

Campaign to Protect Rural England
Tel. 020 7981 2800
www.cpre.org.uk

English Heritage
Tel. 0370 333 1181
www.english-heritage.org.uk

Forestry England
West of England Regional Office
Tel. 0300 067 4800
www.forestryengland.uk

Independent Hostels
Tel. 01629 580427
www.independenthostels.co.uk

Long Distance Walkers' Association
www.ldwa.org.uk

National Trust
Tel. 0344 800 1895
www.nationaltrust.org.uk

Natural England
www.gov.uk/government/organisations/
natural-england

Ordnance Survey
Tel. 03456 050505
www.ordnancesurvey.co.uk

Ramblers
Tel. 0207 339 8500
www.ramblers.org.uk

South West Coast Path Association
Tel. 01752 896237
www.swcp.org.uk

Youth Hostels Association
Tel. 01629 592700
www.yha.org.uk

Text:	Sue Viccars for the South West Coast Path and chapter opener introductions. Original route text supplied for Pathfinder® Guides: *Exmoor & the Quantocks* by Brian Conduit and Sue Viccars; *North and Mid Devon* by Sue Viccars; *Cornwall* by John Brooks and Sue Viccars; *South Devon & Dartmoor* by Brian Conduit and Sue Viccars; and *Dorset and the Jurassic Coast* by Dennis and Jan Kelsall
Photography:	John Brooks, Brian Conduit, David Hancock, Sue Viccars and Kevin Freeborn. Front cover: © Helen Hotson/Shutterstock
Editorial:	Ark Creative (UK) Ltd
Design:	Ark Creative (UK) Ltd

ISBN: 978-0-31909-113-5

First published 2011 by Crimson Publishing and reprinted with amendments in 2019.

This edition first published 2021 by Trotman Publishing.

Trotman Publishing, 19-21D Charles Street, Bath, BA1 1HX
www.pathfinderwalks.co.uk

Printed in India by Replika Press Pvt. Ltd. 3/21

Front cover: Old Harry, off The Foreland, on the Jurassic Coast near Studland, Dorset
Page 1: The Coast Path between Trevone and Stepper Point, North Cornwall

Ordnance Survey

Pathfinder® Guides — Britain's best-loved walking guides